Libraries Designed for Kids

Reference

The Internet

Library Cards

Storytime

NOLAN LUSHINGTON

Neal-Schuman Publishers, Inc.

New York   London

Published by Neal-Schuman Publishers, Inc.
100 William St., Suite 2004
New York, NY 10038

Printed and bound in the United States of America.

The paper used in this publication meets the minimum requirements of American National Standard for Information Sciences-Permanence of Paper for Printed Library Materials, ANSI Z39.48-1992.

Library of Congress Cataloging-in-Publication Data

Lushington, Nolan, 1929-
    Libraries designed for kids / Nolan Lushington.
       p. cm.
    Includes bibliographical references and index.
    ISBN 978-1-55570-631-9 (alk. paper)
    1. Children's libraries—Administration. 2. Young adults' libraries—Administration. 3. Children's libraries—Planning. 4. Young adults' libraries—Planning. 5. Library planning—United States—Case studies. 6. Library architecture. 7. Libraries—Space utilization. 8. Children's libraries—Activity programs. 9. Young adults' libraries—Activity programs. I. Title.

Z718.1.L87 2008
025.197625—dc22

2008032537

Table of Contents

Preface

Libraries Designed for Kids is a one-stop resource for both architects and librarians seeking to create new and exciting libraries for children. As such, it is intended to serve three critical purposes:

1. Guide to the planning process
2. Manual for planning a children's library
3. Reference book for specifications and details critical to effective library design

Years ago, we thought of children's libraries as merely scaled-down adult spaces. Today's younger generations are fortunate to instead have wonderfully conceived and built libraries planned exclusively for them, such as the following:

- The Experience Library in Cerritos, California, that emphasizes the tactical experience of using a library
- The San Francisco Exploratorium and the Queens Borough Public Library, New York, both of which seamlessly integrate hands-on exhibits into the fabric of a children's library
- The Family Place Library initiatives across the country that emphasize family use by welcoming parents and caregivers to share the library experience with their children
- The ImaginOn in Charlotte, North Carolina, that features creative experiences involving the five senses
- The Robin Hood school libraries in New York City that show how small budgets in the hands of innovative architects can make libraries exciting places by featuring the letters and words of students

These model libraries take vastly different approaches to serving the needs of our youngest users, yet each brilliantly meets the library mission.

Libraries Designed for Kids can be used by school and public librarians to design new or adapt existing spaces to better serve today's and tomorrow's generations of young learners. Architects will find interesting ideas as well as practical information to implement exciting new experiences.

Organization of This Book

The organization of this book parallels the planning and design phases of creating a new library space. We begin with conceptualization and evaluation. The Introduction establishes the need for library spaces to be designed especially for children. Chapter

1 describes major innovations in children's library design concepts that were incorporated into several specific library systems and discusses the special design considerations of school libraries. Chapters 2 and 3 outline steps in the evaluation and planning processes and show how to determine the size needs for delivering effective children's services in communities of different sizes.

Design details are addressed next. Chapters 4 and 5 emphasize important design features in general. Chapters 6 through 9 discuss the design concepts related to the functions of the different spaces within the children's area. This part of the book shows, for example, how the spaces for younger children should differ in design from the areas for older children and young adults, how multipurpose areas can be designed to accommodate diverse programming, how staff and storage areas can be effectively integrated, and how to select the appropriate furnishings and equipment for the different areas. Chapters 4 through 9 are structured both for general reading and for use as a ready-reference source for specifications.

Chapter 10 discusses "quick fixes," helpful when there are minimal resources available to address space problems and design mistakes.

The appendices will be useful from initial planning through moving in. Appendix A shows how children in focus groups talk about their own library needs. Appendices B and C present two case studies, one for renovation of a small library and one for designing a large, new space. The annotated readings listed in Appendix D provide the reader an opportunity to further explore the subject. Appendices E and F, which list suppliers and architects, respectively, are a handy reference to support the design and implementation stages.

The most important aspect of a children's library is the opportunity it provides librarians to motivate children to love books. The physical design of the space can support this by centering the design on the staff and on the beautiful books. As children learn to use the library on their own, a good design will make the process easy and interesting and therefore successful. These two elements—staff effectiveness and children's self-service—should be the guiding principles that shape the design.

Acknowledgments

I would like to acknowledge a wide variety of people who have helped to make this book possible.

My wife Louise Blalock worked for many years as a children's librarian and was invaluable in the editing process. Children's librarians in Hartford, Simsbury, Avon, and Middletown, Connecticut; Queens, New York; Bath, Maine; and Hershey, Pennsylvania, and dozens of other libraries contributed to my knowledge of how children use libraries. Peter Gisolfi, Jeffrey Hoover, Elizabeth Martin, Tony Tappe, Stew Roberts, Rick Schoenhardt, Bill Connor, Kevin Hom, and Juergen Riehm, to name just a few of the architects with whom I have worked over the years, have helped to shape my thinking on design issues. The Harvard Graduate School of Design's Public Library Workshop has annually given me an opportunity to listen to the dialogue between architects and librarians.

My associate Mary Beth Mahler has been invaluable in going over the manuscript and suggesting changes as well as taking photographs.

Barbara Joslin of JCJ Architecture supplied the wonderful drawings to illustrate room layouts.

Cindy Guthrie kindly read the manuscript and made many useful comments.

Ace Library consultant Anders Dahlgren was an invaluable reader.

Juergen Riehm of 1100 Architect and Peter Magnani and the staff of the Queens Public Library were an inspiration in the design of that facility.

Charles Harmon of Neal-Schuman Publishers has been patient and persistent.

INTRODUCTION

Improving Service by Design

This book is intended to help children's librarians improve their services by improving their facilities. The overriding theme of *Libraries Designed for Kids* is the idea that children need to be encouraged to make their own choices about what to read in addition to being guided to appropriate books by knowledgeable librarians.

Last November, I heard an inspiring talk given by Cristina Garcia, author of *Dreaming in Cuban*. She said, "There is no more devoted a reader than a ten-year-old that has found a book they liked." *Libraries Designed for Kids* discusses how to create a place where this happens often, where the young reader and the book can be connected.

I have six grandchildren, and I am encouraged about how this generation relates to libraries and books. My grandchildren are all avid readers with very different reading tastes. The champion reader in the family is Olivia Barber, who has read every Harry Potter novel six times. She is so obsessed with books that when she gets off of her school bus to walk the two blocks home, the first thing she does is take a book out of her backpack to read so that she doesn't miss a moment of reading time. She idolizes her school librarian, Mrs. Rabinowitz, because she finds books that Olivia likes. Olivia's major complaint about libraries is that they don't make it easy for kids to find books because there are so many categories. Libraries that split up their collections into chapter books, science project books, picture books, tall books, and other categories that do not suggest the subject matter are often frustrating for children seeking to find a book on a particular subject or by a particular author.

Another granddaughter, Caitlin Lushington, was preparing a research paper on her favorite actress, Audrey Hepburn, so I went with her to her local public library in a small town. We arrived a little before closing time, and the librarian was busy reading at the reference desk when we walked in. When he finally looked up and noticed us, Caitlin asked him for material on Audrey Hepburn. He asked her, "Have you tried the Internet?" Caitlin explained that she had searched the Internet, but she thought the library might have some additional material. He suggested looking in the catalog. By this time I was both disappointed with and furious at his lack of interest. Caitlin and I walked over to the Performing Arts section in the 790 area where we found two books, the Biography section where we found an additional book, and the Reference section, where we found an article in *Current Biography*. All of this material enriched her paper, and she enjoyed the process of thinking through the array of subject areas where she might find materials.

This story illustrates how the opportunity for physical activity in libraries can enhance the library experience. Caitlin learned that a variety of research approaches can yield a greater richness than staring at a screen. Library facilities need to be designed with attractions and guides that encourage users to roam about in the rich library environment, hunting and gathering information from a variety of places in the library.

Not Just Information

People sometimes confuse information bytes with knowledge. The Internet provides access to data and information but seldom has the impact that comes from spending ten hours reading a book. Immersing oneself in a period of history, an extended journey to a foreign country, or a real or fictional life story makes the library experience more powerful than acquiring a byte of information. If every seat in a library was an Internet terminal that was in use the entire time the library was open, this use would amount to only one-tenth of the time users spend reading books they borrow from the library, acquiring knowledge, not just information.

Children differ from one another and change with lightning speed, so children's libraries need to be very different places from adult libraries. Children's libraries need to offer alternating environments that respond to children's varying needs. In addition to the internal flexibility afforded by mobile furnishings, children's libraries should offer exciting busy places as well as calming places of refuge.

The Value of Libraries for Children

Defining moments in the intellectual lives of children occur each time they select a book they want to read. Often these moments occur at a children's library. They may result from a librarian taking an interest in nurturing the natural curiosity of a child. A child's imagination may be captured by an intriguing display of the front cover of a picture book. The vital element of these moments is that the act of selecting the book involves the child (see Juan's Story).

Juan's Story

As they walked into the library Juan felt Grandma Louise squeeze his hand. He was amazed at all of the colorful books in brightly lighted bins. He stopped in front of a book that had a large cat on the cover with a very funny-looking tall hat. He lifted the book out and tucked it under his arm as Grandma led him to a cozy corner up a small ramp where they could snuggle into a large armchair. Grandma would turn the pages of the book as she read the story about the cat in the hat. Occasionally Juan would look up from the book and see other kids playing with the large toys, reading, or looking at computers.

When Grandma had finished the story, Juan climbed down from her lap to play with the other children. Grandma walked over to her friend Alicia, and they sipped coffee and shared the latest news. After a while, all of the children gathered around the librarian to hear a story.

Just before Juan and Louise left the library for lunch, Miss Perez helped Juan choose his very own book that he could take home to read. He chose a Spanish story, because his mother likes books in Spanish and she would be happy to read it with him when she came home from work that night.

Children using libraries frequently find out how they can make the organization of the library work to satisfy their own interests. They begin to understand that the library is arranged to bring together material on their favorite subject and even that the subject has a numerically sequenced Dewey Decimal code that assists them in finding what they want. Understanding library organization allows children to learn to control the library (see Johnny's Story).

Johnny's Story

Johnny could hardly wait for boring school to be over. He would hurry to the public library down the street where he could explore the books on space flight that he had just discovered.

He had been coming to the library for some time now, but the last time he came Miss Perez had shown him that the numbers on the spines of the books could lead him to other books on the same subject. Now he noticed the big numbers and their related subject names over the shelves. Miss Perez explained to him what the numbers meant and made sure that the book Johnny picked out was interesting and readable.

Johnny could also sit down at one of those new cool electronic workstations with the chairs on wheels that can go up or down to fit him perfectly. Johnny liked the book/electronic combo because the books told stories about all kinds of space flight adventures, while the computer helped him to understand some of the new words and to find more information on his special subjects. Miss Perez also showed him how to download magazines onto his iPod.

The magic in reading comes from inside the child. The connection between word and brain image creates a special relationship. Good children's library design results from librarians, planners, and architects working together to create a place that will nurture that imaginative special relationship (see Jim's Story, next page).

The International Federation of Library Associations (www.ifla.org) identifies the essential ingredients of a child's successful library experience:

> Children of all ages should find the library an open, inviting, attractive, challenging and non-threatening place to visit. Ideally, a children's service needs its own library area, which must be easily recognisable (e.g., special furnishings, decorations and colours) and distinct from other parts of the library. Libraries offer a public space where children can meet each other or can meet others in cyber-space.

A variety of studies demonstrate the effectiveness of libraries in children's educational experiences. In her definitive and classic study *Summer Learning and the Effects of Schooling*, Barbara Heyns (1978) followed sixth- and seventh-graders in the Atlanta public schools through two school years and the intervening summer. Key findings of her research include the following:

- The number of books a child reads during the summer is consistently related to his or her academic gains. Regardless of level of family income, children who read six or more books over the summer gained more in reading achievement during the study period than did children who read less.
- Use of a public library during the summer is more predictive of vocabulary gains than attendance at summer school.

Jim's Story

Jim was a children's librarian who had worked in several libraries that were full of books and uncomfortable chairs, but this new library where he had come to work last week was very different. For the first time, he had his own work space where he could prepare his displays and story programs. The staff chairs were mobile and comfortable, and he could adjust the seat to the right height for his computer.

The customer service location had collaborative oversized electronic workstations where he could work with up to three children to do searches. Rather than having to work at a large service desk, staff wore Vocera speakers hanging from neck straps to communicate with other staff as they freely moved around the room helping people. Jim liked this, especially as a new librarian, because as he worked with children he could also talk with Miss Perez about some of the newer search techniques that the library was using.

Book stacks were low, providing staff with views everywhere in the room so that they could easily spot users who needed help. The stacks were also on wheels, so they could easily be reconfigured. Any materials not immediately available physically could be downloaded electronically.

Computers for staff and children were available both as stand-up units in the book stacks for easy lookups and in comfortable workstations. Next to each computer were some book displays that changed every week.

There were group study rooms for parents and caregivers and for students studying and working at computers together. The area for younger children had lots of book displayers and room for children to move around. Parents and caregivers could relax nearby on comfortable chairs with low tables, drink coffee, and chat about their children.

The older children's area had group study zones and more books in low stacks interspersed with interactive exhibits. One exhibit showed the children how scientific principles worked by letting them generate electronic waves, and another one illustrated the relationships among the planets and stars.

The program rooms were fully equipped with overhead projectors and stackable chairs that could be stored out of the way. A special crafts room had folding tables, a counter with a sink, and ample storage space for craft materials. Impromptu storyhours could be easily held in a separate small story area. A computer learning lab was available both for training sessions and for additional workstations when classes were not being held.

- The major factors determining whether a child read over the summer were the following:
  - Whether the child used the public library
  - The child's sex (girls read more than boys but also watched more television)
  - Socioeconomic status
  - Distance between home and a library

According to Heyns (1978: 77):

> More than any other public institution, including the schools, the public library contributed to the intellectual growth of children during the summer. Moreover, unlike summer school programs, the library was used by over half the sample and attracted children from diverse backgrounds.

Drs. Donna Celano and Susan Neuman (2001) describe the ways in which public libraries foster literacy skills through summer reading programs and preschool programs:

- Libraries continue to play a major role in fostering literacy, especially among those most needing assistance in developing literacy skills (e.g., preschool and elementary school children).

- Children who have been exposed to library preschool programs showed a greater number of emergent literacy behaviors and pre-reading skills than those in a control group.
- Children who participate in summer reading programs benefit from the many literacy-related activities offered, aiding significantly in literacy development.
- Public library preschool and summer reading programs encourage children to spend a significant amount of time with books.

Celano and Neuman (2001) studied four groups of children who had low reading scores and who came from low-income working families. Two of the groups attended summer reading programs, and the other two attended day camps. After a few weeks in the programs, the children in the summer reading program read significantly better than those who attended the day camp.

Stephen Krashen (1993) identified the following benefits of voluntary reading programs:

- Reading programs encouraged children to spend increased time with books.
- Public library reading programs played an important role in the reading achievement of children who lack access to books and other reading materials.
- Literacy-related activities and events enriched reading experiences, encouraging children to read themselves, listen to stories read aloud, and write about what they'd read.
- Public library programs encouraged parents to become involved in children's reading.
- Reading as a leisure activity is the best predictor of comprehension, vocabulary, and reading speed.
- Skill-based reading exercises (in two studies) did not help comprehension levels. Outstanding high school writers reported extensive summer reading.
- The positive relationship between free voluntary reading and literacy is extremely consistent, even when different tests, different methods of reading habits, and different definitions of free reading are used.
- If children read one million words a year, at least one thousand words will be added to their vocabulary. One study found that this could easily be accomplished by letting children and teens chose any format of reading material they wanted, including comics. Studies also showed that spelling improved with increased reading.

Krashen and Shin (2004) studied the differences in reading gains among children of families in different income brackets. They found that free voluntary reading resulted in improvement in the following areas:

- Reading comprehension
- Writing style
- Vocabulary
- Spelling
- Grammar usage

These improvements were in contrast to poor results from direct reading instruction! From my personal experience, I have seen that increasing access to books and reading through various summer library programs garners tremendous benefits, particularly for children of lower-income families.

As part of a larger reading initiative in Southern California, many public libraries together sponsored the Library Summer Reading Program in 2001. The program was designed to increase children's summer reading. The following results were reported (The Evaluation and Training Institute, 2001):

- Ninety-eight percent of the participating students reported that they liked the program.
- Ninety-nine percent reported that they liked going to the library.
- There was an 11 percent increase in the number of parents reading to their children more than 15 hours per week.
- Before the summer, 77 percent of parents reported that their child read 9 hours or less per week.
- The number of children reading 10–14 hours per week increased 9 percent, and the number of children reading 15 or more books per week rose 11 percent.
- Fifty-five percent of participants had a high enthusiasm for reading compared with less than 40 percent of nonparticipants.
- More participating than nonparticipating students performed at or above grade level in word recognition, reading vocabulary, and reading comprehension. Student perceptions concurred with teacher reports.

In summary:

- Research shows the public library summer reading program enhances student achievement—even when compared to direct instruction.
- Research studies and experiences with promoting summer reading have shown how essential are the partnerships between schools and public libraries.
- Because research strongly supports free voluntary reading, as practiced in most public library preschool programs, it is recommended that state and federal funds be used to support preschool programming in public libraries.

Two further studies are noteworthy. The Urban Libraries Council (2007) studied the relationship between public libraries and economic development. It concluded, "Early literacy initiatives promote reading, prepare young children for school and raise levels of education." In 2005, a study commissioned by the Pennsylvania Department of Education's Office of Commonwealth Libraries (Griffiths, King, and Aerni, 2006) showed that libraries return almost five times their cost. Other findings include the following:

- People spend thousands of hours reading, listening, and viewing free library materials that would otherwise cost them millions.
- Early childhood educational development saves communities millions by avoiding the need for remedial educational programs.

- Public libraries engage teenagers and create communities of learning and enjoyment that avoid many teenage community problems.
- Homework helpers give valuable assistance with school projects.

Adopt-a-Library Literacy Program

I was asked to speak at the Nova Scotia Library Conference in 2007 and had the good fortune to be driven to the conference by Constable John Kennedy of the Royal Canadian Mounted Police. In the course of the trip, he told me a story about how he became interested in the power of public libraries. He was patrolling in a small town in New Brunswick when he spotted some teenagers skateboarding in front of the library. He noticed that although they liked that spot for skateboarding, they never entered the library, so he stopped and asked them why they were never in the library. They answered that the library had no books. He was puzzled by their reply so he invited them to come into the library with him, and he then realized that what they meant was that there were no books in the library that interested teenagers.

John then went to the local school and asked the principal to let him work with the child who had the worst attendance record in the school. When John met and interviewed the boy, John found out that his ambition was to become a truck driver. John bought him a toy truck, placed it in the principal's office, and explained that the child would get the truck if he improved his attendance and started reading.

John then began a campaign to get vendors to contribute books to the library that teenagers would be more likely to enjoy, such as comic books and graphic novels. At the same time he came across statistics that showed that people in jail were overwhelmingly illiterate. He began thinking that a good way to reduce crime would be to encourage kids to use public libraries. He widened his campaign to get books.

John founded the Adopt-a-Library Literacy Program (www.fightingcrime.ca). He soon enlisted the Royal Canadian Mounted Police and the Pictou-Antigonish Regional Library (in Nova Scotia). Now, public libraries, police departments, and local businesses as well as organizations and private individuals work together to raise money for new books. The purpose is to provide community places and activities to discourage violence and drug use. John also started a reading contest, the Reading Challenge, on the Web site. Prizes are awarded to celebrate the world reading championship as a means to motivate local libraries to get their communities reading.

The Adopt-a-Library program promotes the concept of literacy and crime prevention and helps to communicate ideas and opportunities to members and sponsors. All members are free to develop their own strategies based on local needs and directions. A common strategy used by several police agencies and libraries involves the following steps:

1. Police contact local businesses to support literacy as a means of crime prevention.
2. Items donated to libraries are used as prizes to encourage children to read.
3. Donations support summer reading programs.
4. The number of children participating and the number of books they read are tracked as a way of measuring the local impact.

What Draws Children to Public Libraries?

On January 22, 2008, an article in *USA TODAY* quoted a Harris Interactive (2007) online survey of 1,262 youth ages 8–18 conducted June 13–21, 2007 (margin of error 3 percent):

- Seventy-eight percent borrowed items for personal use.
- Sixty-seven percent borrowed items for schoolwork.
- Thirty-four percent read books in the library.
- Thirty-four percent used the Internet for research.
- Twenty-six percent studied.
- Twenty-five percent used computers for fun.
- Twenty percent attended events held at the library.

These results show that most children who visit the library do so to borrow items for personal use. Additionally, the survey shows that a large percentage of children also visit the library to gain access to computer-related services.

This rich mixture of books and computers is an essential element in the design of libraries. Successful children's library designs in the twenty-first century will do the following:

- Give children a choice when selecting their own materials to take home.
- Provide a comfortable place to use computers and do homework.
- Provide a variety of attractive programs.
- Support the work of talented and well-trained children's librarians.

People love stories told in all formats, from puppet shows to pantomimes, films, videos, DVDs, and large-format picture books. The importance of visual aids should not be overlooked when designing libraries for children.

One of the first children's public libraries was initiated by Caroline Hewins in Hartford, Connecticut, just before the turn of the twentieth century. Caroline was a remarkable pioneer in many areas of library service. She had a collection of dolls that she used with children, and she wrote a book about what children read in the 1850s when she grew up. She also worked with families in Hartford boarding houses. Like all great children's librarians, she understood that libraries are about stories. Her library encouraged families and children to see dolls as visual aids to storytelling.

The covers of picture books encourage children to read. The American Library Association (ALA) recognizes the importance of pictures by giving awards not only for books but also for the pictures that accompany them. The Caldecott Medal, named in honor of nineteenth-century English illustrator Randolph Caldecott, is awarded annually by the Association for Library Service to Children, a division of the ALA, to the artist of the most distinguished American picture book for children.

Encouraging children to use libraries by designing beautiful and nurturing places that welcome them, and their parents and caregivers, to a lifelong experience of the world of books and electronic resources is the most effective way of ensuring a future population of well-informed, intelligent, and productive citizens. The studies cited in this introduction show the value of reading for children. Key findings are that voluntary reading is more useful than summer school and that public libraries foster learning in preschool children. Children's libraries at their best celebrate reading with displays of words and pictures.

References

Celano, Donna, and Susan B. Neuman. 2001. *The Role of Public Libraries in Children's Literacy Development: An Evaluation Report*. Harrisburg: Pennsylvania Library Association. Available: www.statelibrary.state.pa.us/libraries/lib/libraries/Role%20of%20Libraries.pdf (accessed May 2008).

Evaluation and Training Institute. 2001. *Evaluation of the Public Library Summer Reading Program: Books and Beyond . . . Take Me to Your Reader!* Final Report to the Los Angeles County Public Library Foundation. Los Angeles: Evaluation and Training Institute. Available: www.colapublib.org/about/Readingby.pdf (accessed May 2008).

Garcia, Cristina. 1992. *Dreaming in Cuban*. New York: Ballantine Books.

Griffiths, Jose-Marie, Donald W. King, and Sarah E. Aerni. 2006. *Taxpayer Return-on-Investment (ROI) in Pennsylvania Public Libraries*. Chapel Hill: University of North Carolina. Available: www.statelibrary.state.pa.us/libraries/lib/libraries/PAROIreportFINAL7.pdf (accessed May 2008).

Harris Interactive. 2007. *American Library Association Youth and Library Use Study*. New York: Harris Interactive, Inc. Available: www.ala.org/ala/yalsa/HarrisYouthPoll.pdf (accessed May 2008).

Heyns, Barbara. 1978. *Summer Learning and the Effects of Schooling*. New York: Academic Press.

International Federation of Library Associations. *Guidelines for Children's Libraries Services*. Available: www.ifla.org/VII/s10/pubs/ChildrensGuidelines.pdf (accessed May 2008).

Krashen, Stephen. 1993. *The Power of Reading*. Westport, CT: Libraries Unlimited.

Krashen, Stephen, and Fay Shin. 2004. "Summer Reading and the Potential Contribution of the Public Library in Improving Reading for Children of Poverty." *Public Library Quarterly* 23, no. 3/4: 99–109.

Urban Libraries Council. 2007. *Making Cities Stronger: Public Library Contributions to Local Economic Development*. Evanston, IL: Urban Libraries Council. Available: www.urbanlibraries .org/files/making_cities_stronger.pdf (accessed May 2008).

1
Innovative Children's Library Models

This chapter identifies revolutionary design concepts that evolved at different times. It then examines current models of children's library design that demonstrate the various ways in which the design of the library works to achieve the ultimate goal of fostering greater learning and growth in children. The chapter ends with a discussion of the special design considerations for school libraries and school–public library combinations, how these differ from those for public libraries, and the basic space guidelines for media centers in these situations.

Nineteenth- and Twentieth-Century Libraries

Architecture tells stories, and designs for children's libraries demonstrate how our society views children. When children's library spaces were first designed, in the late 1800s, they tended to mirror the design of libraries in general—walls of books surrounding chairs and tables, with a librarian's desk near the entrance to the area.

As the number of books published increased, the physical layout of libraries evolved into book stack areas with freestanding shelves and narrow aisles. There would be a reading room nearby with smaller child-sized tables and chairs. Eventually, story rooms were added, and some evolved into multipurpose rooms with a small stage for puppet shows and an area for crafts.

Libraries changed in the 1980s with the introduction of new media formats. New types of shelving appeared to accommodate videos and cassettes, and displays changed also to better feature the front covers of picture books. Libraries underwent further changes in the 1990s as computers became more accessible and electronic resources, such as educational software programs and the Internet, became available.

Twenty-First-Century Libraries

Now, in the twenty-first century, children's library design has expanded to include a wide variety of functional concepts to satisfy the needs and wants of children. Design teams now use many different methods to create effective children's libraries. Results vary from bland, traditional, book-filled, junk shop–type libraries with nothing but seats and books to WOW and Experience libraries (examples of which appear in following sections), which may be closer to Disneyland than to library land.

How do these new design concepts encourage connections between children and the imaginative world of books? They combine elements to nurture connections.

Family Place Libraries

The Family Place Libraries model focuses on providing a nurturing family experience for children (www.familyplacelibraries.org/aboutUs.html):

> The Family Place Libraries initiative began in 1996 when Libraries for the Future (LFF) was searching the nation for a model parent program in a public library. A visit to Middle Country Public Library (MCPL) and the Parent/Child Workshop sparked this collaborative project. "We knew enough to say this is different," says Diantha Schull, LFF's former president. "It really met a community-collaborative need."
>
> Working together, LFF and MCPL refined the workshop's principles and developed a framework for a replicable model to show all libraries a new way to look at children's services. The newly dubbed *Family Place* library kept the Parent-Child Workshop as its cornerstone, but built a structure around it comprised of key core elements to expand the role of public libraries as community centers and key players in family and early childhood development, parent and community involvement and lifelong learning beginning at birth. With a grant from the Hasbro Children's Foundation in 1998, the initiative was launched at libraries in five communities: Harford [*sic*] (CT), Baltimore (MD), Lyndonville (VT), Providence (RI) and Centereach (NY)
>
> The first Family Place Training Institute, based upon a new interdisciplinary training curriculum, was offered in 1999. Since then 435 librarians from 25 states have attended the Training Institute and joined the national network of Family Place Libraries. (see also Sonenberg, 2005; www.lff.org)

Family Place Libraries (www.familyplacelibraries.org) focus on early childhood and parent services featuring emergent literacy and family support principles and practice, including:

- Using and borrowing library materials
- Playing and interacting with parents and other adults
- Engaging in learning activities
- Connecting with families of varying ages, stages, and cultures
- Engaging in conversation with one another and library staff

Sandra Feinberg and colleagues (2007) wrote in *The Family Centered Library Handbook* about ways of creating family spaces within libraries and their benefits. Family-centered libraries encourage play, interactive learning, and socialization. Feinberg et al. (2007) recommend that designers "sit on the floor and look around to achieve a young child's perspective on the library" (p. 97).

Proponents of family-centered libraries feel that nooks, crannies, and partial enclosures are appealing to very young children. Young children prefer to play in small groups of two to five, so the part of the library devoted to them should provide a variety of large and small, active and quiet areas. This will allow children to choose their own environment, yet caregivers can easily monitor their activities. Young children love mobility, and exhibits that move are especially attractive. Proponents recommend making boundaries with fish tanks or low shelving to help preserve visual sight lines.

Children's libraries should be designed for children and adults together (Feinberg et al., 2007). Family place library design integrates comfortable adult seating into the children's area with provision for caregivers to talk with one another while keeping an eye on their children. Finally, proponents discourage the concept of permanently themed areas, which may in time become boring and dated.

Robin Hood Libraries

The Robin Hood Foundation was established in 1988 to fight poverty in New York City, and it has provided funding for run-down elementary schools. Volunteer architectural teams create newly designed and furnished elementary school libraries. Recently, one of these libraries won the American Institute of Libraries and American Library Association award for the best library designs in the country. These libraries often celebrate words and books in their designs. A wonderful Robin Hood project led by Henry Myerberg used children's poetry as its decorative feature on the walls (see Figure 1-1).

Figure 1-1
Interior walls decorated with poetry at a Robin Hood Foundation (NY) school library, designed by Henry Myerberg of HMA2 (photo by Peter Mauss of ESTO).

The Robin Hood Foundation works in partnership with the New York City Department of Education to reconceive libraries in public schools. By transforming these libraries into active learning centers, the foundation hopes to address both low literacy and weak student performance among children from lower-income households. By

> [w]orking with schools in high poverty neighborhoods that have low academic achievement, the partners are committed to fundamentally transforming school libraries into vital resources for the whole school community—students, teachers, and parents—that will impact and contribute to improved student performance. (www.robinhood.org/programs/initiative_details.cfm? initiativeId=4)

The Robin Hood Foundation's Library Initiative attracted much support from major donors, including funding and donations (totaling $40 million) to cover the costs of the initiative's efforts, from architectural services to new computers. Another partnership with Syracuse University's Master's of Library Science Program provided training for elementary school librarians.

> The first 10 libraries of the Initiative were completed in fall 2002 in Harlem, the South Bronx, Brooklyn, Queens and Staten Island. Twenty-one more libraries opened throughout the city in fall 2004 [and] twenty-five more libraries will be reinvented. (www.robinhood.org/programs/initiative_details.cfm?initiativeId=4)

Cerritos, The Experience Library

The Cerritos Library in California, designed by Charles Walton and Associates (Glendale, CA), represents a whole new approach to library design:

> The new $40 million library. . . is the first titanium-clad building in the United States, with a golden skin that changes color with atmospheric conditions. . . . [It] is the culmination of [ideas] . . . [i]nspired in part by the book *The Experience Economy* [Pine et al., 1999]. [A] planning team of City elected officials and Library staff, architects, artists, designers, contractors and consultants redesigned every aspect of the Library with the goal of enhancing the user experience. . . . (www.ci.cerritos.ca.us/library/childrens.html)

This "Experience Library" offers themed spaces that highlight its different collections, such as the Old World Reading Room (first editions, collectible books, popular books) and the World Traditions area (non-English multimedia resources). The library has greatly increased its collections in support of its vision of books as "essential learning tools for the twenty-first century." Technology provides support for both library functions and services and user experiences:

> [T]he library's intranet . . . allows individual users to customize the display of electronic resources [and] features extensive locally developed content. Multimedia learning centers reinforce the importance of books and reading by combining print materials with Web resources, in-house original content, and the latest in computer graphics. Public areas house 200 computer workstations and seating with 1,200 laptop ports. (www.ci.cerritos.ca.us/library/childrens/html)

The Cerritos Library's Children's area, the design of which is based on the concept of "save the planet," features a made-to-scale rainforest and a planetarium. Other educational exhibits include:

- A life-size Tyrannosaurus Rex replica named "Stan"
- The "Spirit of Cerritos," a scale-model NASA space shuttle
- A lighthouse
- A 15,000-gallon saltwater aquarium
- A rainforest tree to demonstrate the rainforest's healing properties and how trees help clean the air
- A geologic core model with strata depicting eras of geologic time
- A sky painted on the ceiling to show different atmospheric conditions (www.ci .cerritos.ca.us/library/childrens.html)

The Cerritos Library also features many other innovations added specifically for children, such as electronic and learning center resources, "spontaneous programming," arts and theater, foreign-language children's books, and so forth—all designed to make Cerritos Library a "learning destination." Some specific child-inspired innovations follow:

- A blue screen featuring scenes from literature next to the entrance, used for taking photographs of children during special events
- A reference desk labeled "Help" in a kid-friendly, animated area
- A computer workstation area
- Interactive and educational CD-ROM products
- Spontaneous programs, for example:
  - "Meet at the Tree"
  - "Facts About Dinosaurs"
  - "Deep Space"
  - "Creatures of the Rainforest"
- Planned programs, for example:
  - Pajama Night
  - Saturday Morning Story Hour
  - Family Night
  - Babies and Books
  - Child and Teen read-aloud activities
  - Computer classes
  - KeyPals (e-mail pen pals)
  - Arts and crafts
  - Holiday programs
  - Tours for classes (www.ci.cerritos.ca.us/library/childrens.html)

WOW and GASP Libraries

In South Africa the "WOW" idea has been defined as a complex effort to establish branding through a planning process. Kathy Kunneke (2007), of the University of South

Africa, Pretoria, explores the "WOW library" concept in detail in her paper "Creating and Marketing a WOW-Library." The principle is to establish a unique identity for the library and then market it as if it were a "brand."

Another brand-creation strategy, called GASP (graphics, ambiance, style, presentation), based on a marketing initiative in the hospitality industry, is used by the West Palm Beach (Florida) Public Library. The goal is to define an identity for the library that is then used to develop an overall concept that guides the re-creation process:

> This concept is unique to a particular library, product or company. This concept is then used to guide all decision making in creating spaces, selecting colors, lighting, materials, integrating interior furnishings, graphics, style of services, and programs. . . . [B]y defining the desired characteristics of a library personality, decisions regarding space planning, furnishings, and services adhere to a specific integrated vision . . . [allowing the library to] undergo an interior makeover and invigorate its programs and services in a cohesive manner. (www.wpbpl.com/gasp.php)

ImaginOn

In Charlotte, North Carolina, a children's library was combined with a children's theater to create the ImaginOn:

> Bob Cannon, the former Executive Director of the Public Library of Charlotte & Mecklenburg County (PLCMC), and Bruce LaRowe, Executive Director of Children's Theatre of Charlotte (CTC), each led organizations with great programs for young people . . . and both were running out of space.
>
> Bob and Bruce thought it would make sense to consider creating a new, shared facility, to meet the growing needs of both organizations. (www.imaginon.org/about_imaginon/default.asp)

Based on their shared mission of "bringing stories to life," Bob and Bruce created a space where "young people [can] learn in many ways, through all five senses and 'from the page to the stage.'" The two partnering organizations, the CTC and the PLCMC, are innovative and active in their community and offer a variety of programs for young people (preschool to late teens) and families:

- CTC's popular program areas:
  ○ MainStage productions
  ○ Tarradiddle Players, the professional touring company
  ○ Community Involvement Program
  ○ Education classes for both the community and the schools
- PLCMC's innovative programs:
  ○ The award-winning Novello Festival of Reading, a celebration that accentuates reading and learning with authors
  ○ The Gaming Zone, a video and tabletop program for all ages
  ○ The World Language Center, which extends access to language instruction materials (www.imaginon.org/about_imaginon/default.asp)

The Children's Library Discovery Center

Tom Galante, Peter Magnani, and the staff of the Queens Borough Public Library, working with Juergen Riehm and his team at 1100 Architect in New York City and Tom Rockwell of The Exploratorium (a science musuem in San Francisco), have designed and created the new Children's Library Discover Center in Queens, New York. The project is managed and executed by the Libraries Unit of the New York City Department of Design and Construction, and the design is meant to showcase the library's presence and contribution to the community:

> The 21,000 square foot Children's Library Discovery Center [consists] of two stories.…The exterior shell is comprised of four types of glazing ranging from transparent, translucent, opaque and opaque with texture, with High Performance glazing used at all transparent and translucent openings. The glowing glass facade, analogous to the "Jewel Box," is elemental in increasing the library's visibility in the surrounding community and reintroducing it as a central cultural and social destination. . . . The completed project is expected to receive the Leadership in Energy and Environmental Design (LEED) Silver rating. (www.1100architect.com/ work.php?category=8)

This project recently won an Excellence in Design award from the Art Commission of the City of New York.

Several views of the Children's Library Discovery Center are shown in Figures 1-2 through 1-4 (and others are included in Chapter 5). We discuss the concepts incorporated into this library more fully in Chapter 7 under Designing for Older Children.

Alcove Libraries—Amsterdam (Netherlands) Public Library

Jo Coenen's design of the basement children's area features curved subject alcoves with soft seating surrounded by books. This idea of a book-filled, sheltered reading area (see, for example, Figure 1-5) has been one of the cornerstones of library functional

Figure 1-2
External view of the Children's Library Discovery Center in Queens, New York, designed by Juergen Riehm of 1100 Architect.

Figure 1-3
Book stacks in the Children's Library Discovery Center.

Figure 1-4
Floor map incorporated into the innovative design
of the Children's Library Discovery Center.

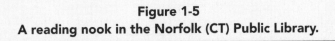

Figure 1-5
A reading nook in the Norfolk (CT) Public Library.

design for hundreds of years. It dates back to the early monastery libraries of Europe and is frequently seen in American public libraries of the nineteenth century, such as Richardson's design for the Woburn (Massachusetts) Public Library. Coenen achieves a comforting reading atmosphere amid stacks of books with a modern look that includes curving white stacks and colorful soft chairs (for pictures of Coenen's work, see www.designws.com/pagina/1bibliotheekadam.html).

According to Stephen Krashen (2004: 63), "The physical characteristics of the reading environment are important" because "preschool and kindergarten children used the library corner more when it had pillows, easy chairs and carpets and when it was partitioned off and quiet" (citing the work of Morrow, 1983).

Sustainable Design—Green Libraries

Green library designs incorporate an array of techniques to conserve resources, reduce operating costs, and create healthy library environments. It is vital for children to experience the children's library as an example of this Green Philosophy so that children experience libraries as places that conserve resources and are healthy environments.

What Is LEED?

The Leadership in Energy and Environmental Design (LEED) Green Building Rating System is "the nationally accepted benchmark for the design, construction, and operation of high performance green buildings," as defined by the U.S. Green Building Council (www.usgbc.org/DisplayPage.aspx?CategoryID=19). "LEED provides building owners and operators with the tools they need to have an immediate and measurable impact on their buildings' performance."

Reading areas with green plants and indoor gardens as well as outside views of plants and trees can give children a sense of nature as well as improve indoor air quality. The LEED system promotes a whole-building approach to sustainability by recognizing performance in five key areas of human and environmental health:

1. Sustainable site development
2. Water savings
3. Energy efficiency
4. Materials selection
5. Indoor environmental quality

When the Clifton Park–Halfmoon Library, in Clifton Park, New York, needed to expand its facilities, the Board of Trustees decided to "go green." In 2004, the trustees began working with Bill Connors of the Woodward Connor Gillies & Seleman architectural firm to create what they hope will be a LEED-certified facility. The new building, which opened in 2006, exemplifies many of the green issues and has reduced operating costs by $60,000 per year compared with other similar-sized facilities. (Visit the library's Web site at www.cphlibrary.org for more details.)

School Libraries

According to Peter Gisolfi (1998: 35) in his article "A Place to Read":

> To integrate the library fully into the educational life of an elementary school,
>
> 1. Locate the library centrally within the school
> 2. Provide separate areas for different functions
> 3. Design the entire space so that it can be observed by one adult
> 4. Incorporate computers seamlessly into the library environment

My experience as the librarian at St. Andrews School in Middletown, Delaware, which became famous as the site for the Robin Williams film *Dead Poets Society*, as well as my experience in running the elementary school libraries in Greenwich, Connecticut, taught me the differences between school and public libraries.

How School Libraries Differ from Public Libraries

Most of the material covered so far in this book also applies to the design of school libraries. However, there are some important differences. Many of these differences relate to the requirement that school libraries support the curriculum of the school in addition to encouraging students to use the library to pursue noncurricular interests. In addition, the entire library needs to be constructed with special sound-absorbent materials, with particular attention paid to glass walls that amplify sound, so as not to disrupt activities outside or within the library.

To support curriculum activities, the library should have enough space for classroom-sized groups to use. English teachers may want to bring their entire class together in the library when they are teaching about how to research a paper. Geography and history teachers often assign group projects and could arrange for their students to work together in the library.

Having sufficient chairs and tables to accommodate a class while allowing space for individual library use is a design issue. Should there be complete acoustical separation with the class held in an adjoining room so that class activities do not conflict with individual use? Or should the class have the opportunity to see and use the entire library space during classes? In this case, the library needs to have an area with acoustical dampening or separation by book stacks or some other sound-absorbing technique.

The need to work with classes as well as individual students in the same library room often causes conflicts because the two uses interfere with each other. Therefore, it will be important in the design to separate these two functions with walls or with acoustically absorbent furnishings such as book stacks.

Librarians and teachers will often work together in preparation for a class visit. Librarians may be asked to create curriculum-related displays of materials on mobile display carts that can be easily moved and changed. To work with teachers in a school library, librarians need a location in their work area for consultations during preparation for a special class activity.

Studies have shown that children who select their own books are more successful in school, so giving students an opportunity to pick out their own books is an important element in the design. This may be achieved by displays of books with their attractive front covers showing. Making the stacks self-service with clear signs indicating the subjects and their Dewey Decimal numbers helps students to find topics of interest to them. Students need to receive individual assistance from the librarian, in marked contrast to the class activity, which provides little opportunity for individual interaction with staff.

Large collaborative electronic workstations that make it possible for librarians and students to look at the same computer screens are a design feature that encourages this individual interaction. A service desk with a separate chair for students is another way of offering this service.

Children often work together on projects, so it is helpful to have grouped study areas, such as mobile chairs and tables, that can be reorganized to accommodate changing group sizes. Small rooms designated for group study may also be helpful. These rooms should include power and communication receptacles for computers as well as tack boards so that students can share their ideas. Glass doors allow easy monitoring of these rooms.

Librarians must be able to turn the library into a computer classroom with overhead projection and electronic workstations for each student. Media production facilities are seldom found in public library children's facilities, but they are much more common in school libraries.

Elementary School Libraries

Typical elementary school libraries are often small rooms with a few books and chairs. Wonderful exceptions are the libraries created by the Robin Hood Foundation, described earlier in this chapter (www.robinhood.org/programs/initiative_details.cfm? initiativeId=4). The partners work together to design and build exciting new elementary school libraries in high-poverty neighborhoods (see Figure 1-6). The Robin Hood Libraries celebrate language by displaying letters and their meanings and by giving kids an opportunity to study actively in small groups as well as quiet nooks.

High School Libraries

Larger high school libraries are sometimes arranged by major subject disciplines, so there will be a science and math section as well as humanities and social science areas. Each one may be separately located and equipped with electronic workstations, book collections, and reference databases and materials in the appropriate subjects.

Public and School Library Combinations

In some communities, public and school library combinations may be a useful idea, but there are a variety of special considerations for this type of library:

- Public libraries need to be located where people go for other purposes, such as retail shopping centers. Schools are often located in low-traffic, out-of-the-way areas that are deserted at night.
- Elderly people may not want to enter a building filled with noisy young people during class visits.

Figure 1-6
Cider Mill Elementary School Library (Wilton, CT), designed by Tai Soo Kim Architects of Hartford, Connecticut.

- School curriculum–oriented materials do not have much interest for many public library users.
- Operating a large heating and cooling system for the entire school to keep the public library open after hours, on holidays, and during summer vacation may not be economical.

Size Recommendations

Kathryn Bugher, the School Library Media Consultant for the Wisconsin Department of Public Instruction, wrote "Design Considerations for School Library Media Centers" in 2006. Within this, Bugher explains how 6 square feet per school student is the general guideline to follow in planning and then offers these specific measurements for the different functional areas:

- Circulation (300–400 sq. ft.)
- General reading/browsing/listening/viewing area (student pop. × 10% × 40 sq. ft./ per student)
- Group instruction (700 sq. ft.)
- Multimedia production/storage (500–700 sq. ft.)
- Processing/work room/office (500–700 sq. ft.)

Bugher then turns her attention to the particulars of shelving calculations (for 3-foot shelves):

- Picture/thin: 20 books per foot/60 books per shelf
- Standard size: 10 books per foot/30 books per shelf
- Reference books: 6 books per foot/18 books per shelf
- Periodicals: 1 per foot for display purposes

She then explains how to calculate the linear feet of shelving required for a given collection—total number of volumes divided by number of books per foot—and offers this example:

> [A] primary collection of 5,000 volumes consisting of picture and thin books would require a total of 250 linear feet of shelving. Remember—shelves should only be two-thirds full. To allow for this, multiply the number of linear feet required by 1.33. Example: 250 × 1.33 = 332.5 or 333 linear feet of shelving.

Chapter Summary

This chapter describes a variety of new library models, from the nineteenth to the twenty-first century, including those fashioned after the green philosophy of sustainable design. Some of the models presented include:

- Family Place Libraries, which emphasize designing the library for use by children with caregivers
- Robin Hood Libraries, which convert elementary school libraries into imaginative new library spaces

- The Cerritos Library, which emphasizes the physical experience of children in libraries
- GASP libraries, such as the West Palm Beach Public Library, which emphasize branding libraries by using techniques initiated in the hospitality industry to assist in creating a brand or an identity
- The ImaginOn in Charlotte, North Carolina, which combines a children's library with a children's theater
- The Children's Library Discovery Center in Queens, New York, which integrates interactive exhibits with library materials
- The Clifton Park–Halfmoon Library, based on green concepts that seek to minimize the impact of the library building on the environment as well as incorporate green plants and indoor gardens to give children a sense of nature

The final section of the chapter focuses on the special design considerations and space guidelines that should be taken into account when designing for a school library versus a public library.

References

Bugher, Kathryn M. 2006. "Design Considerations for School Library Media Centers." Madison, WI: Wisconsin Department of Public Instruction. Available: http://dpi.state.wi.us/imt/desgnlmc.html (accessed May 2008).

Feinberg, Sandra, Kathleen Deerr, Barbara A. Jordan, Marcellina Byrne, and Lisa G. Kropp. 2007. *The Family Centered Library Handbook*. New York: Neal-Schuman.

Gisolfi, Peter. 1998. "A Place to Read." American School Board Journal *185*, no. 10 (October): 35–37.

Krashen, Stephen. 2004. *The Power of Reading Insights from the Research*, 2nd edition. Westport, CT: Libraries Unlimited.

Kunneke, Kathy. 2007. "Creating and Marketing a WOW-Library." Available: www.ifla.org/IV/ifla73/papers/122-Kunneke-en.pdf (accessed May 2008).

Morrow, L. 1983. "Relationships Between Literature Programs, Library Corner Designs, and Children's Use of Literature." *Journal of Educational Research* 75: 339–344.

Pine, B. Joseph, et al. 1999. *The Experience Economy*. Cambridge, MA: Harvard Business School Press.

Sonenberg, Nina. 2005. *Libraries for the Future: Innovation in Action*. New York: Libraries for the Future.

2

Planning a New Children's Library

Children's librarians should understand the entire library planning process to better understand how children's library planning fits into the overall plan for the library. This is important because most children's library planning occurs within the context of planning the entire library. This chapter outlines the planning process for building a new children's library with an emphasis on community-based collaboration. It then examines all of the issues regarding the proposed library design in depth to better understand what is needed to add to an existing children's library or to build a new one.

Brief Outline of the Planning Process

I. **Create the planning team**
   A. Community members
      1. The board of trustees
      2. Committee members
   B. Library staff
      1. Librarians
      2. Support staff
   C. The library consultant
   D. The architect and interior designer

II. **Perform a community demographic analysis**
   A. Education
   B. Population growth
   C. Economics and cultural characteristics

III. **Elicit community input**
   A. Community leaders
   B. Organizations
   C. Focus groups

IV. **Create vision and mission statements**
   A. Vision statement
   B. Mission statement

V. **Analyze the current library facilities and services**
   A. Library facilities
   B. Library services
   C. Perform a needs assessment

VI. **Create the physical building program**
   A. Architectural work
      1. Plans
      2. Equipment
      3. Construction
   B. Interior design

Create the Planning Team

The several members of the planning team will become part of the planning process at different stages, and their roles will change as the process moves forward. The team will include the following:

- Members of the community who are involved in operating and funding the library
- Library staff, including the children's librarian, who initiate the process and serve as the client
- Library users, especially children's caregivers
- Library building consultant, who is familiar with the planning process and acts as the coach (see Appendix B for a case study of the consultant's role in this process)
- Architect and interior designer, who design the facility (see Appendix F for a list of architects)

In a planning process, the relationships among the members of the planning team are crucial to the success of the project. These relationships inevitably and appropriately change throughout the planning stage. In a complex process with several interrelated participants, it is most useful for all participants to be involved early in the project, although the extent of involvement of each team member will change as the project proceeds.

Community Members

The board of trustees or town building committee can help determine the mission and objectives for the project and assist with the library's long-range plan for service improvement and with raising the necessary funds. These people also serve as communicators and liaisons with the wider community. They may work on selecting the architect. The staff, consultant, and architect will then keep the board and community informed of the progress of the project by monthly informational meetings. However, the day-to-day planning will be performed by the staff, the consultant, and the architect working together as a team.

Library Staff

The library staff often initiate the library improvement process by perceiving that the physical facility is beginning to limit the quality of service. This will result from observation, public complaints, and comparisons with other libraries. The staff may then involve the library board and members of the community funding sources. Throughout the project, the staff will work closely with the consultant and architect to shape the planning process and building design and to raise funds.

Library Consultant

A library consultant is an experienced coach familiar with the process who knows about the alternatives. A consultant will teach about users and buildings, frame the process, supply knowledge of the details, improve the product, and hopefully save the client money. The consultant works with the staff to evaluate the existing children's library space in light of the library's overall mission. This evaluation then becomes the basis for building objectives to improve the ability of the library to deliver the variety of services desired.

The consultant writes the building program with staff assistance. The consultant's most important role is in the review of plans at the schematic phase of design to ensure that library program requirements have been met.

To find a consultant, you can begin with the list maintained by the Library Administration and Management Association (a division of the American Library Association). You must first register to access the list (available at https://cs.ala.org/lbcl/search/); depending on the level of access you want, you may also have to pay a fee. Alternatively, talking with colleagues about consultants may be a better way of finding one.

The process of selecting and retaining a consultant often begins with a Request for Proposals for Consultants, which should include the following:

- Description of the project
- Mission and vision statements
- Request for consultant qualifications
  - Master of Library Science
  - Experience as a library director and public service librarian
  - Experience as a building consultant
  - Fee and expense parameters

Interview consultants by touring the library with them and listening to their questions and comments about the building. Does the consultant listen to you and respond with thoughtful comments and questions about the library and its services? In addition to the library tour and interview, you should base your selection on the experience and recommendations of the consultant's former clients.

The Architect and Interior Designer

The architect designs the library based on input from the community members, library staff and patrons, and library consultant. The architect is involved in four phases:

1. Creating the schematic design, showing furniture and equipment relationships
2. Assisting in design development, including mechanical systems
3. Providing construction drawings and specifications to show the contractor how to build the library
4. Supervising construction to ensure that the contractor follows the plans and specifications

The interior designer works with the architect, consultant, and library staff to select and install the furnishings required by the program. Interior designers will know what types of chairs and shelving, for example, will create a nurturing environment for children that will foster learning and also where to obtain them.

Perform a Community Demographic Analysis

A demographic analysis studies those factors that most affect library use. Basic population growth will affect future library use and should be studied in detail, including estimating trends for the next 20 years.

Education

The community's average education level may be the best indicator of a library's use for populations of similar size. Better-educated people will use the library more often than an undereducated population; therefore, a community with a highly educated population may require a larger facility.

Community census reports include the percentage of people over 25 years of age who have completed high school or college. Comparing this with similar state or national statistics may be useful in determining the types of services most needed. A community with a low percentage of graduates may have a great need for early childhood education programs and literacy classes, whereas other communities would benefit more from computers that contain sophisticated software programs.

Population Growth

Compiling a demographic profile with projections of the growth of the town for the next 20 years will be useful. The library staff can obtain local data from:

- Town or city planning departments
- Regional planning agencies
- State planning agencies
- School districts
- Utility companies

Obtaining more than one estimate allows comparison. It may be helpful to investigate the accuracy of prior predictions by finding predictions for the past 10 years and comparing them with the actual figures.

The most useful statistics compare changing demographics and library use over time within the town itself. For example, a library with a new building in 1980 and a population of 20,000 may have grown in population by 10 percent by the year 2000, but library use may have increased by 50 percent and the educational attainment may have changed from 75 to 85 percent high school graduates. These changes may signal a greater need for expanded facilities than a town with a more consistent population growth and library use.

Economics and Cultural Characteristics

Median family income levels and percentage of employment may affect library space and service needs. If there is a high level of unemployment, many people may come to the library for information on employment and job skills. These people would benefit from access to employment agency databases and online continuing education courses.

An understanding of the cultural characteristics of the local community is also important. If the community has traditionally been composed of Hispanics, with many books by Hispanic authors, and a significant number of African Americans or Eastern Europeans have moved into the community in the past ten years, they may find little to interest them in the library.

Elicit Community Input

Listening to people talk is an important part of the planning process because it involves individuals directly in the process. It is far more important than making presentations to community groups to try to persuade them to follow particular recommendations. Listening honors the opinions of the speakers, especially if their opinions become part of the planning process. Active listening means responding to the ideas of the listeners rather than arguing with them or trying to change their point of view.

When listening to the community, we often hear complaints about the library that may be painful to the library staff who work so hard to deliver good services. The Zen saying "An enemy is better than a Buddha" is helpful in understanding that complaints about the library are useful. Too often, library users become tolerant of poor conditions. This may be a result of the library's limited resources. The staff should welcome complaints as useful guides for improvement. Staff sometimes take complaints as personal criticisms or pass them off as examples of administrative failure on the part of the bosses. Complaints should be recorded in writing by the staff and a written response forwarded by the administration. If complaint books are used, the response to the complaint should appear in the book.

Complaints can, in fact, be a positive indicator when viewed as an expression of caring about the library and the staff. If users were indifferent, they would not take the time to discuss their concerns. Listening and responding respectfully to both the positive and negative comments will go a long way toward developing the friends and allies needed.

Community Leaders

One-on-one meetings with community leaders provide an opportunity to discover their attitudes toward the library. The meetings may result in suggestions for improving library services, as well as assessments of fund-raising potential. Library administrators have an opportunity to inform community leaders that the library is planning to improve and to solicit support for library plans. Community leaders include the following:

- Public and private school officials
- Parent–teacher organization members
- Political, governmental, and financial planners
- Potential fund contributors
- Communication leaders (e.g., those managing local radio and television stations)
- Organization leaders (e.g., members and directors of local Rotary, Kiwanis, and YMCA groups)
- Clergypeople and union representatives
- Government employees, including those working in the areas of health and human services and parks and recreation

Organizations

Because the library staff interact with and respond to users' needs on a daily basis, the staff can help identify specific library services that will support the goals and aspirations of local community organizations, including the following:

- Local Head Start programs, daycare facilities, family groups, and caregivers might benefit from more information about early childhood education and child development.
- Cultural or ethnic organizations or a local literacy council might benefit from activities such as cultural literary events and reading tutorials.
- Local employment agencies might better serve their clients if they could count on the local library to offer some computer training.
- The local chapter of the American Cancer Society or Juvenile Diabetes Foundation might benefit from specialized medical collections.
- Genealogy clubs could benefit from specialized local history resources.
- New groups in the community, for example, new immigrant groups might benefit from the development of programs on citizenship requirements.

Interview teachers and other group leaders who bring large groups to the library. They will identify changes in the community, such as a new downtown revival effort or increased ethnic diversity, that result in further special needs to consider.

Library trustees and members of a library's Friends group have useful information about the community:

- The history of library improvement efforts
- Movers and shakers in the community
- Community organizations for collaborative efforts
- Constraints on library improvement activities

Schedule meetings with community organizations for help not only in planning but also in building community support. Community organizations will identify library needs in the populations they include or serve and can develop support for library capital funding. Involve representatives of groups and agencies early in the planning and make their needs part of the facility improvement program. Coming to community organizations for support after the library is planned will lead to lukewarm interest compared with involving them early in the planning process. Be sure to include the following organizations early:

- Head Start and other preschool program caregivers for children can be strong advocates for the expansion of children's facilities to include children's meeting and program space and tutorial facilities.
- Ethnic organizations will support the library's need for literacy tutorial space and foreign language collections, including music and videos.
- Health care agencies will support the library's efforts to inform the community about health information topics. Libraries can partner with health care agencies to help train mothers to give their babies a physically, mentally, and emotionally healthy start.

- Realtors will support an improved library because it enhances the quality of life by encouraging and stimulating the intellectual and cultural community.
- Educational institutions will support the expansion of the library's facilities to benefit their students' work. However, beware of the potential competition with the board of education for capital expenditures, and be prepared to fight for the library's fair share of long-term capital expenditures.
- The community governing body and fiscal authorities should also be involved in preliminary planning so that the library can be assured of financial resources.

Focus Groups

Focus groups of children, parents, and caregivers provide planners with an opportunity to listen to what users want to see in the library. Convening focus groups of staff or library users will be helpful in determining perceptions or attitudes (discussed also in Chapter 3).

Select focus group members from among the library's users. Do not include those who might dominate or inhibit an open exchange of ideas. Trustees, town employees, taxpayer groups, and relatives of staff and trustees may have strong biases that might inhibit discussion, and therefore they should not be included either. A trained discussion facilitator will encourage open discussion.

Staff focus groups often concentrate on staff facilities, complaints about temperature fluctuations, and working conditions. Encourage staff to also discuss library public service needs and improvement objectives. Staff might know about common questions asked by the public relating to the building design:

- Are children confused about how to find books?
- Can children find a quiet place to study?
- Can users easily find the children's and program rooms?
- Are there frequent complaints about noise?

Beware of assuming that the focus group accurately represents the community. Focus groups suggest ideas that can then be tested with a survey. To measure community opinion, a random sample telephone survey will be more accurate than a focus group. A written survey distributed to users in the library will also help determine community perceptions or attitudes toward the library.

Create Vision and Mission Statements

Vision Statement

A vision statement is a vivid description of a desired outcome. Because it also reflects the values of the organization, it usually has more emotional content than a mission statement. Library vision statements often focus on the look and feel of the library services.

Mission Statement

A mission statement defines an organization's purpose and objectives. A library's mission involves providing a service to the community and should not only reflect the history and traditions of the library but also look forward to opportunities to improve and increase the use of library services. Good mission statements also include a goal to work toward.

Review the mission statement every five years, but if it continues to be relevant, it can remain unchanged for some time. A broad and concise mission statement will allow more specific service responses to be built on this mission foundation. Some late-nineteenth-century mission statements have survived well into the twenty-first century. For example, the mission of the Greenwich, Connecticut, library for 100 years was "the promotion of useful knowledge." According to this mission statement, this library's role is to encourage use, not just provide materials. This library has a broad concern with knowledge rather than a narrow focus on information or materials.

Sample Visions, Missions, Goals, and Objectives

The following is an example of a brief statement:

Vision:

The Public Library will be a dynamic place promoting the love of knowledge and the joy of reading.

Mission:

The Public Library connects individuals with resources in order to enhance lives and build community.

Goal:

The Public Library will promote early literacy through programs, services, and collections that meet the personal, informational, and recreational needs of children from birth through kindergarten, their caregivers, and their families.

Objectives:

Objective 1: Stimulate the growth of reading skills by offering supporting services and programs.

Objective 2: Select, maintain, and promote reading, viewing, and listening materials appealing to a variety of interests.

Objective 3: Offer staff training on early literacy principles and on the skills required to deliver programs and materials to young children and their caregivers.

Objective 4: Increase community awareness of the importance of early literacy experiences and the resources available at the library.

Objective 5: Provide an appealing, engaging, and safe environment.

Objective 6: Build relationships with community groups that serve preschool- and kindergarten-age children.

The following is an example of a longer, more traditional statement:

Vision Statement

Residents will have the opportunity to use a variety of services that reflect the community's wide-ranging interests and needs. The library will strengthen and continue successful existing services and develop new initiatives designed to broaden the library user base.

Residents will have opportunities to attend and participate in an array of programs sponsored by the library and local organizations, as well as public meetings held at the library, to enhance their involvement in community life and their connections to fellow residents. The library will increase attendance and expand participation in such events to attract people to become library users and supporters, thereby enriching their lives through this experience.

The library will provide full access to resources and services to meet residents' educational, informational, and recreational needs. This will be accomplished through a variety of means, including:

- Providing convenient, comfortable, and inviting facilities with appropriate technology capabilities for individual and group use
- Providing adequate, accessible, and convenient parking and access to the building
- Extending evening and weekend hours of operation to increase opportunities for residents to use library services at their convenience
- Providing a spectrum of multilingual services to enable residents to use library and community resources

Mission Statement

The Public Library will be a leader in promoting reading, literacy, and lifelong learning for all generations and provide materials, services, and programs to meet the community's diverse informational and recreational needs. To fulfill this mission, the library focuses on providing the following:

General Information

Resources and services to answer residents' informational questions on a broad array of topics related to work, school, and personal life

Emergent Literacy by Creating Young Readers

Preschool programs and services designed to ensure that children will enter school ready to learn to read, write, and listen

Current Topics and Titles

Resources and services to enhance residents' leisure time; to meet the demand for users' recreational reading, viewing, and listening interests; and to help users make choices from among the options

Lifelong Learning

Resources and services to explore topics of residents' personal interests and to support lifelong learning pursuits

Community Spaces

A safe, comfortable, and welcoming physical space for residents to meet and interact with other people or to sit quietly and read and open and accessible virtual spaces that support social networking among residents

Analyze the Current Library Facilities and Services

This process is at the heart of planning. It shows how the community looks and works. Understanding the community and how the library responds to community needs will affect the success of the improvement project.

Library Facilities

Walking around, driving around, and observing people may provide some useful clues:

- Is there pedestrian traffic past the library?
- Is the library located near schools, playgrounds, or athletic fields that may result in a major influx of children at a particular time?
- Are there homeschool activities that may require special staff effort?
- Will children and caregivers have special needs?

Suburban libraries far from pedestrian traffic might give more thought to implementing drive-up service or to making the library more attractive from the parking lot side. Ideas on how to improve the outside appearance of the library might come from competing establishments such as bookstores or from display strategies used in other retail outlets.

Urban libraries may need to make a greater effort to enhance their street presence. Affixing an iconic symbol, perhaps a giant graphic, or at least a large, lighted sign can help remind people passing the library about what is happening inside the library.

Library Services

USAGE STATISTICS AND PATTERNS

The library staff and consultant need to determine changes in library services. They can analyze library use statistics and output measures for past years, especially for the year of the last facility improvement. Book circulation, reference use, program attendance, and in-library use are considered.

Library use statistics have evolved considerably in the past 20 years. Now libraries routinely measure not just library circulation but library visits, program attendance, reference questions, and in-library use. Use of computers in the library is of primary importance in needs assessment. Success in obtaining needed materials and answering questions is also measured.

Outcome measures and the balanced scorecard model seek to determine the effects of library use by interviews with users and exit interviews of children leaving the library. Robert Kaplan and David Norton first introduced the idea of a Balanced Scorecard in 1992 in *Harvard Business Review*. They developed the Balanced Scorecard "to identify a set of measures that reflect future performance to compliment [*sic*] the backward-looking" financial measures ("Balanced Scorecards: A Primer," 2004, p. 1). Thus, the objectives and measures for the balanced scorecard are chosen from an organization's vision and strategy and include financial, customer, internal process, and innovation and learning (sometimes called *organizational readiness*).

How do these statistics affect library space planning? Compile them into a chart for use as a visual aid. A demonstrated increase in library use can be a powerful argument for the need for more space. Also compare these data with state and regional averages.

Consultants can also study use of library services by interviewing library staff, who can report on the extent and rhythm of their activity and space needs and reveal their attitudes toward new technological options for service delivery. The consultant should observe library services and staff activities to verify user and staff perceptions and interview nonusers to determine the potential for increased use by assessing their attitudes and perceptions.

Observing how children behave will help librarians to frame their guidelines for design professionals:

- Do children mostly select books from displays or bins, or do they go to the conventional book spine-out shelves?
- Do children select books by finding subjects?
- Do middle schoolers congregate in one particular part of the library, or are they spread out in all areas?
- Do children come mostly with parents/caregivers, or do they come alone?
- Are children mostly noisy and active, or do they also seek quiet corners?
- Do children do homework mostly in groups, or do they study alone?
- Are children waiting to use computers?

LIBRARY COLLECTIONS

The responsiveness of the collection to children's needs is more relevant than sheer numbers of materials. In fact, many libraries that reduce the size of their collections by removing little-used materials find that their collection use increases because the users' perception is that the collection is more relevant to their needs. Providing access to the Internet and electronic databases along with downloading capabilities may reduce the need for book and magazine space but will require more space for electronic workstations.

BEHAVIOR MAPPING

Behavior mapping describes the relative functions of various spaces within a building (discussed also in Chapter 3). It can therefore help consultants and librarians understand the relative use of different parts of the library over a period of time. Library behavior-mapping studies determine the kinds and frequencies of use of the services offered. This technique also records the use of library furnishings and equipment.

Prepare a map showing the locations of tables, lounge chairs, study carrels, electronic workstations, stand-up work desks, computers, listening or viewing stations, book stacks, and staff service desks. Studies done under my supervision recorded the date and time at the top of the map, and at each hour the number of users at each location is recorded on the hourly map. At the end of a week, the hourly maps are studied to compare the use of tables versus lounge chairs versus carrels, and so forth, at various times.

Relative overall activity in each area of the library can be used to schedule staff in the busiest locations. Equipment types and quantities can be reorganized. Library users are observed browsing new materials, searching the book stacks and media materials, asking questions of library staff, studying reference and class materials, reading newspapers, books, and magazines, and using computers.

Katherine Silbereis, at the West Hartford (CT) Public Library conducted a behavior-mapping study in 2003 and recorded the following observations (unpublished):

- The most frequent activities were using the computer (for Internet access and otherwise), reading, and studying. The busiest time was 1:00 p.m.
- Some anecdotal observations were made. On the day of the study (which was conducted during the summer season), most nonfiction browsers were noted perusing the biography and memoir sections rather than the mezzanine area.
- A nearly equal number of patrons perused the fiction stacks and new book area initially, but the statistic sharply rose in favor of the new book area at 1:00 p.m.
- Most patrons came alone and preferred to be by themselves at a four-seat table. They also used a study carrel or lounge seat. Sixty-four percent of total library patrons seated on this day were by themselves at a four-seat table.
- More people were browsing than using computers, but computer use was the largest single use and probably limited by the number of computers available. If the numbers of people reading magazines, newspapers, and books were totaled, it would be larger than the number of people using a computer or browsing.
- Teenagers were spotted playing video games in addition to using the Internet.
- Many teenagers and younger adults studied reference or class materials of their own.
- A majority of the patrons seated appeared to have come alone. Most also appeared to be settled for awhile. The teen room is by far the most social room. Many teens came in small groups or ran into acquaintances.

TRACKING STUDIES BY TRAINED OBSERVERS

Paco Underhill's decades of research into retail shoppers' behavior (reported in his 1999 book *Why We Buy*) is an example of how observation of user behavior can improve interior design. He has performed such a study for the San Jose (CA) Public Library (Underhill, 2007). A trained observer knows about different ways in which users behave and can think creatively about choices. Observers must be both experienced about libraries and creative about solutions. Trained observers in libraries can spot the favored study locations and consider the combinations of ambiance, furnishings, lighting, and spatial relationships that affect these locations. Trained observers have seen different libraries and understand how library space problems can be solved.

Tracking studies determine how people respond to the building:

- How do people travel through the building?
- Where do they stop?
- What do they do?
- Will children borrow more picture books from face-out bins or from spine-out divider shelves?

Observing library users clustered around terminals with printers may suggest that more printers or more efficient methods of delivering copies to users are needed.

For observation to yield useful results, the library must provide choices in its existing facility, and observers must be experienced with potential patterns of library user behavior and alternative responses to that behavior: A choice of seating may yield the need for more table or lounge seats, whichever is used the most. Offering users a choice of computers on tables or embedded terminals will show which they prefer.

Perform a Needs Assessment

A needs assessment study is an in-depth analysis of the current situation. Its purpose is to identify what the specific needs are so that improvements can be made. It is an important process when analyzing the current library services and facilities and is discussed in detail in Chapter 3.

Create the Physical Building Program

Architectural Work

Once the current library services and facility have been analyzed, the planning team develops a program describing how the library should work. This program guides the architect in developing plans.

First, the architect sketches out each part of the children's library showing the furniture and equipment layout. The plans are then reviewed by staff and the consultant to verify that capacities for seating and materials meet program requirements.

The architect then adds details regarding lighting, heating and ventilating, and air conditioning for each area. Once these have been completed, a more detailed construction document is created. These are the architectural plans the builder will follow. The architect remains involved during the building phase to supervise the construction and the installation of furniture and equipment.

Interior Designer

The architect works with the interior designer before finalizing the architectural plans. The interior designer will have discussed in detail with the library staff and consultant what types of furniture, shelving, and workstations should be included to meet the new service goals.

A Streamlined Approach to Planning for Small Libraries

Some libraries may find the following condensed steps useful when planning changes or designing new spaces:

- Form a planning committee, including community members and organizations:
  - ○ Town government officials
  - ○ Potential contributors
  - ○ Local service groups and schools
  - ○ Friends of the library and avid users
- Select a library consultant to guide the planning committee through the remaining steps.
- Develop a fact sheet about the community and the library showing:
  - ○ Existing library services
  - ○ Population projection for the next 20 years

- ○ Library activity for the past 10 years
- ○ Library history
- Define current conditions in the library and conduct a SWOT analysis:
  - ○ Strengths
  - ○ Weaknesses
  - ○ Opportunities
  - ○ Threats
- Orient planning committee (who, what, why, when) and set a timeline for the process.
- Determine community vision.
- Select library service responses and link to community needs.
- Write mission statement.
- Determine goals and objectives—specific objectives for services and facility.
- Conduct needs assessment.
- Write building program.
- Hire architect to design project.
- Determine resources required—budget, staff, maintenance.
- Write communication plan and obtain funding.
- Create architectural plans, design the interior, and build the structure.
- Perform postoccupancy evaluation—a year after the building opens, the planning team and additional experts should evaluate how the plan was carried out and make changes to reflect new uses of the library.

Chapter Summary

This chapter outlines the planning process with an emphasis on community-based collaborative planning. Community and library concerns are the basis for developing the building program, which delineates specific space needs, describes space relationships, and recommends furniture and equipment. This chapter provides sample mission, vision, goal, and objective statements and discusses how to evaluate community and facility needs. Sample programs are provided in Appendices B and C.

References

"Balanced Scorecards: A Primer." 2004. Carlsbad, CA: City of Carlsbad, California. Available: www.carlsbadca.gov/imls/documents/scorecards.doc.

Kaplan, Robert, and David Norton. 1992. "The Balanced Scorecard: Measures That Drive Performance." *Harvard Business Review* (January–February): 71–80.

Underhill, Paco. 1999. *Why We Buy*. New York: Simon & Schuster.

Underhill, Paco. 2007. *San Jose Public Libraries and Hayward Public Libraries: Final Report*. New York: Envirosell. Available: www.sjlibrary.org/about/sjpl/sjway/SVPL-HPL_final_report.pdf.

3

Assessing Physical Needs

This chapter outlines methods for formulating library service objectives based on the community planning processes discussed in Chapter 2. It shows, based on the author's experience, how to evaluate existing space, capacity, and size requirements to assess what is actually needed to build a children's library.

The first, preliminary estimate of space needs will seldom remain unchanged. As librarians, consultants, and architects work through the planning and actual building and furnishing stages, the estimate will be refined before the actual size of the finished area is decided. Further planning will include a more accurate listing of all items of equipment, and architectural design will refine space needs. However, the first rough estimate will be useful for discussions of size and costs with funding authorities when seeking needed resources. For the preliminary estimate, round the numbers off to a slightly larger rather than smaller amount because the various groups that review the plan will be more likely to decrease the size than to increase it.

Major improvements in a library facility will result in changes in use. This will affect space needs in different ways:

- Borrowing: As borrowing increases, less shelf space will be needed for materials in the building.
- In-library use: As more people use technology to access digital information, more space will be needed for workstations.

Consultants work with the staff to determine specific space needs:

- Analyze community library service needs as described in Chapter 2.
- Observe library users.
- Evaluate existing facilities.
- Compare with situations in other communities.
- Set objectives.

The librarian takes the lead in this phase, with the consultant coaching the librarian by suggesting the framework for the process: evaluate facilities by staff interviews and consultant observation and compare existing children's facilities with other similar children's libraries. The librarian often initiates the planning process by becoming aware of these factors:

- Children's materials are crowding out users.
- Children are waiting to use a computer terminal.
- There is not enough space for children attending storyhours and other programs.
- There is no quiet area for study.

State grants, private donors, and budget surpluses may provide opportunities for action. Collaboration with other agencies may suggest space needs and opportunities.

Facility Evaluation

This section includes a number of techniques with which to evaluate current facilities. Facility evaluation should begin with focus groups—a staff focus group and a user focus group.

Focus Groups

Form two focus groups, one of library staff and one of library users. Each group discusses what is good and bad about the present library facility. The following lists indicate the kinds of problems and solutions that may be identified from focus groups.

- What staff like about the children's library:
  - There is a separate story and craft area with storage, sink, and bathroom.
  - With the separate, well-defined areas, noise and activities are contained within each area.
- What staff dislike:
  - The service desk is placed so that at times people enter the space from behind the staff. The two entrances—staircase and ramp—make it hard to face two directions at once so that we can adequately greet users.
  - Picture books are too far from the service desk.
  - We hate the central barrier of an air-handling unit that dominates the entrance to the room.
  - We need a pegboard wall for puppets and bags.
  - The paperback shelves need a backing so that books don't fall off.
  - Lighting is often glary in some areas and sometimes insufficient in other areas.
  - The service desk is too large, and it is not ergonomically designed.
  - We need more self-service signage.
- What users like:
  - The quiet study room is isolated from most noisy areas.
  - The service desk is close to the computers.
  - The play area and picture books are together and close to the family bathroom.
- What users dislike:
  - Computers are not separate from the homework study area, so kids doing homework hear the computer noise.
  - Occasionally there is an unpleasant gasoline smell from outside.
  - Picture books are too far from the service desk.
  - The chairs are uncomfortable.

     ○ There aren't enough printers for each computer terminal, so we have to wait a long time for our turn to print something.

     ○ The book stacks are too tall. My child can't reach most of the books.

     ○ The small play area with a view out into the courtyard is nice but too small, and children may get lost running into the courtyard when the door is open.

Studies and Comparisons

Maximum use studies determine times when there is a maximum use of library facilities. Chart specific times and determine percentage of maximum use compared with total open hours.

Compare services, capacities, and holdings of the existing library facilities with library standards. There are few national standards, but many states have building standards. Also compare the current facilities with those in surrounding communities that serve similar populations.

Study collection–use relationships. Compare the use of various segments of the collections with the amount of materials and the annual expenditures in these segments. Document the inadequacies of the building for handicapped accessibility, materials storage, public service, staff work space, and public safety. This is accomplished by detailed measurement of the areas and capacities for materials and seating.

Population standards are generally outmoded and much less useful than examining each community's unique community requirements. However, these standards have been used for decades and are still quite common in some states. Public libraries were often sized according to population served. These standards are based on the democratic assumption that similar-sized towns should have access to similar-sized educational resources. Common recommendations for smaller libraries, those serving towns of 10,000 to 50,000 people, include the following:

- One square foot of building space for each person served
- Three to five books per capita
- Five seats per thousand population

Gather and analyze library visitation statistics. Libraries differ widely in how intensively they are used. A library that has 500 people a day entering the building will have markedly different space requirements than a library with 800 people a day coming in the front door, even if both serve the same size population.

Intensity-of-use measures affect space needs. For example, in-library use measures the extent of use of library materials *in* the library building, which in turn may affect the need for additional seating. Behavior mapping can determine how frequently seating and other facilities are in use, thereby indicating how many additional seats may be needed.

Objectives

Once mission and role priorities are established, the library staff may develop objectives to improve services. Children should be able to:

- Browse through new materials easily, quickly, and comfortably
- Find a book quickly and easily by author, subject, or title
- Study comfortably and quietly for a long period of time
- Get professional library assistance quickly and easily
- Enjoy a safe and secure environment in the library
- Engage in craft activities
- Attend a storyhour
- Watch a puppet show

Parents and caregivers should be able to:

- Read to children quietly
- Browse in parenting materials
- Observe their children easily

Children's library staff should:

- Have a dedicated work and storage space
- Be able to observe children easily
- Be able to assist children with using computers

Therefore, examples of objectives for the children's area include the following:

- More space for quiet study and for computer use
- Better arrangement of service desk in relation to entrance
- Picture book and larger play area for younger children that are closer to staff and to the family bathroom
- Clear passages and continued definition of various activities
- Wider aisles
- Improved lighting for books and people
- Wide, accessible entry

Determining Adequate Space

In my experience, the total area for children's services generally varies from 20 to 40 percent of the library's total assignable area. A basic preliminary space estimate of future needs is based on the objectives and determines the overall size of the children's library by looking at the capacity requirements for materials and seating, programs and staff, and storage. This estimate is then further refined by a careful analysis of each functional area.

There are several major areas for children:

- Collection space to hold materials for public use
- People space to play, move around, read, and use computers
- Networking and socialization space
- Parent/child space for children and caregivers to be together
- Meeting space for craft or story programs, tutorials, and group study
- Staff space for public service and staff work
- Storage

Collection Space and Material Storage

To determine the number of years before additional shelf space is needed, count the number of existing empty shelf spaces and compare with the annual net additions. Add the size of existing collections plus annual *net* acquisitions for a given planning period, often 20 years. A 10,000-volume library acquiring 500 materials per year and discarding 200 will need space for 16,000 materials in 20 years.

Consider changes in circulation when predicting the need for additional space. Circulation differs from month to month, so there may be plenty of shelf space in January and crowded shelves in June. Improved facilities and more easily accessible shelves can increase circulation, thus reducing shelving needs. Shortening the loan period may increase the circulation.

Frequency of Use

Determine the percentage of the circulating collection that has not been borrowed over a specified period of time—often 2 years. If over 25 percent of the collection has not been used, the library may consider discarding unused materials before determining how much additional collection space is needed. Older collections give the impression that most of the library's materials are out of date, thus discouraging use. Libraries must balance the need for in-depth resources against the need to look up to date.

Library use is changing. Patrons are less likely now to borrow materials they consider out of date. By using specific books, the community is telling the library which books to retain and which are not needed. Gaps in the older materials are relatively easy to locate since the advent of the Internet. The Internet makes it easy to find materials in other libraries that can be obtained through interlibrary loan.

Guidelines and Space Standards

Space standards exist for various library functions. The Library Administration and Management Association's *Building Blocks for Planning Functional Library Space* (LAMA BES Facilities Committee, 2001) includes detailed formulas to help calculate the square footage required for every conceivable element of a library building. In addition, Connecticut and Wisconsin publish planning guidelines that are useful in determining size and capacity standards (see the respective State Library Web sites).

Materials

The following standards can be used to determine if and how many more shelving units may be needed:

- Picture book bins should hold 40 books per running foot.
- A double-faced bin unit will house 250 picture books.
- Book stacks for fiction and nonfiction are often 60 inches high with 40- to 48-inch aisles, accommodating 300 to 350 books per 3-foot section and allowing 10 to 15 books per square foot of floor space.

- Media can be accommodated in regular adjustable book stacks with special shelves for different kinds of media that hang on the same uprights. These can include bins for DVDs.
- Spinner racks are usually to be avoided; they are difficult to sequence, so it is hard to find a particular item. They do hold more items per square foot of space.

The following guidelines may also be used to determine space requirements for books. Variations will occur among libraries because of different shelving policies and mixes of materials. For example, art books take more space if they are kept in sequence, because they are often taller than other books. In general, however, allowing for empty shelf space for reshelving:

Type of Material	Vols./Items per Square Foot of Floor Space	Vols./Items per Linear Foot of Shelf Space
Picture books (in low bins)	20	40
Children's reading books	10	15
Children's reference books	10	7
DVDs and CDs (in bins)	10	20
Periodicals displayed (title)	1.5	1

A quick approximation for a public library assumes ten books per square foot of space. These are preliminary calculations based on 5-foot-high stacks with five shelves and handicap-accessible aisles. Variations in height and aisle width will affect capacity. A stack spacing allowing for a 4-foot aisle and only four rather than five shelves high might better accommodate children. Older parents and caregivers may have difficulty reaching low shelves (LAMA BES Facilities Committee, 2001).

Seating and Electronic Workstations

Five seats per 1,000 people in the community is a useful starting point for determining total seating needs for the entire library. About 10 to 20 percent of these may be in the children's area. It may also be useful to conduct a behavior-mapping study, recording the number of children using seats at particular times, and to experiment with different kinds of seating to see how the different types of seating should be distributed. The following guidelines may be helpful:

- Table seats—35 square feet per seat
- Lounge chairs—40 square feet per lounge chair
- Electronic workstations—40 to 60 square feet per workstation
- Collaborative electronic workstations (where children work together or with staff or parents or caregivers) require more space.

Meeting Space

Space needs for programs, tutorials, and group study vary widely depending on mission and service priorities, but there is a trend toward increased need for meeting space. Generally libraries will try to provide a 30-seat program room for children and additional group study rooms. This may require 500 square feet, including storage space for chairs and tables.

Staff Service and Work Areas

Staff service and work areas will often require 25 percent of the library's assignable space. Needs include:

- Service desks for circulating materials and answering reference questions
- Staff offices
- Storage areas
- Work areas

Do not overlook the need for a sizable work area for children's librarians because children's librarians continuously create and store program displays and storyhour materials.

Nonassignable Space

In addition to space for specific library functions, space is needed for the building's infrastructure. The infrastructure can require from 25 to 40 percent of the total area, depending on the architectural design. Infrastructure includes the following:

- Entrance and vestibule
- Walls
- Restrooms
- Stairs, elevators, and hallways
- Heating, ventilating, and air-conditioning equipment
- Custodial, cleaning, and maintenance equipment
- Delivery area and general storage

Budgetary Considerations

Several budgetary needs may be difficult to predict.

- Maintenance and custodial care: A new building or a major addition may require more or, rarely, less maintenance and custodial care.
- Increased use: A more attractive physical facility may result in increased cost for increased services.
- Consolidation of public service points: Fewer staff service points in a more efficient layout may result in more efficient deployment of staff and lower cost.
- Sustainable building design may reduce operating costs for energy but will add to the construction cost.

Size Estimates and Spreadsheets for a Small and a Larger Library

The following examples are hypothetical estimates for the space needs in two sample towns with populations of 30,000 and 10,000. As discussed at the beginning of this chapter, at this early stage in planning, rough estimates are used to begin thinking of appropriate capacities and sizes. They will later be refined by architectural drawings showing the exact placement of seating, materials, and service areas. These architectural drawings will give a more exact idea of the final sizes and cost.

The preliminary estimate for a children's library in a town of 30,000 people is 5,000 square feet:

50 seats at 35 square feet per seat (average)	1,750
Shelves of assorted styles	2,150
Service and staff accommodations	600
Children's program space for 30 people	500
Total library space	5,000

The preliminary spreadsheet for this children's library (shown in Table 3-1) compares the existing children's library capacities and areas with the proposed new library. The spreadsheet breakdown is based on discussions with the library administration and staff as to the specific functional area requirements. This is still only an approximation, which will be further refined by a detailed analysis of specific furniture and equipment requirements and architectural layouts.

The preliminary estimate of space need for a children's library in a town of 10,000 people is 2,200 square feet:

20 seats at 35 square feet per seat	700
Shelves of assorted styles	1,000
Service and staff accommodations	200
Children's program space for 20 people	300
Total library space	2,200

Table 3-1 Present and projected space usage for a population of 30,000.						
	Present	Present	Present	Future	Future	Future
Library Area by Function	Area	Materials	Seats	Area	Materials	Seats
Children's staff and storage				600		
Young children pic+E+Board	200	100	10	1,650	200	30
Older children and book stacks	500	200	8	1,750	400	16
Audiovisual materials and paperbacks	100	50		500	200	4
Children's programs	200			500		35*
Totals	1,000	350	18	5,000	800	50

Notes: *Program seats are not available for regular library use. Area is measured in square feet; materials in number of shelves; and seats in number of seats.

Table 3-2 Present and projected space usage for a population of 10,000.						
	Present	Present	Present	Future	Future	Future
Library Area by Function	Area	Materials	Seats	Area	Materials	Seats
Children's staff and storage				200		
Young children pic+E+Board	350	50	10	700	200	10
Older children and book stacks	200	100		700	200	10
Audiovisual materials and paperbacks	40	20		300	100	
Children's programs				300		20*
Totals	590	170	10	2,200	500	20

Notes: *Program seats are not available for regular library use. Area is measured in square feet; materials in number of shelves; and seats in number of seats.

The spreadsheet for the larger children's library is shown in Table 3-2. It is preliminary and will change as the planning process progresses.

Chapter Summary

This chapter outlines a method for determining service objectives, evaluating existing spaces, and determining capacity and size requirements for a children's library. Various material and seating standards for converting material and seating count into square feet of building space are shown. Nonassignable space is defined. Two sizes of libraries are compared, with spreadsheets showing capacities and sizes.

Reference

LAMA BES Facilities Committee. 2001. *Building Blocks for Planning Functional Library Space.* Lanham, MD: Scarecrow Press.

4

Design Considerations

This chapter addresses the physical variables that one must consider when designing a children's library. It shows how conflicting design objectives require thoughtful responses. It also discusses the optimum use of the library's space for staff efficiency.

Thinking About Children

To create a place that is useful for a variety of users, the design must achieve a balance between seemingly contradictory requirements:

- The convenience of children and the efficiency of staff
- The needs of young children and the needs of older children and preteens
- Active and exciting open spaces and quiet places to work and read
- Up-to-date technology and familiar furnishings
- Comfortable ambience and good staff supervision
- Help from librarians and privacy protection
- Attractive, efficient design and the potential for expansion
- Natural light and control of excessive heat
- Artificial light and minimal glare

Children's services design must provide for a full range of activities that promote and encourage learning, reading, and the enjoyment of books and other media. Layout and appearance will make a lasting impression on the child. The area should express warmth and friendliness and suggest to parent and child that this is the place to come in order to satisfy both informational and recreational needs.

Services and materials must meet the needs of a range of library users, from the curious preschool toddler to the developing preteen with rapidly changing interests. They must also serve the needs of parents, professionals, teachers, psychologists, and others who will use the collection to support their work with children.

Creative treatment of ceilings, doors, windows, and furnishings should provide a strong immediate message that this is a special place. The character and history of the community, expressed by displays and seasonal decorations, are an important aspect of the children's area. There will be tackable display walls in different parts of the room, as well as display cases.

Indirect and diffuse ambient lighting will impart a quiet and cozy atmosphere by avoiding glare. Adjustable spotlighting for materials and displays will provide strong visual punctuation for materials.

The children's room will have several distinct areas arranged to invite children, parents, and caregivers to move through the space in accordance with the child's conceptual development. Because of the wide range of ages and things done here, there will be a noticeably different ambience for these areas within the larger space. Transitional areas between each of these spaces will house services common to both age groups, such as the computer area between the spaces for younger and older children.

Each of the areas should serve as an imaginal landscape of the developmental period. The space should invoke a sense of creative discovery while also allowing containment for the projection and experience of the child's own imaginal field—a real field of dreams that encourages and supports a variety of imaginative feelings and creative thought.

The sequence of areas should facilitate a successively more introverted relationship to the materials so that the preschool child can be engaged with caregivers and staff while the intermediate child can work more independently in the book and reference areas.

Children grow at varying rates and psychologically change with chameleon-like speed, so pay close attention to these characteristics in the design of the room. Adult designers should try walking around on their knees to get some sense of how children will experience these spaces. Sixty-inch-high book stacks can seem like deep canyons to four-year-olds. Give children the sense that they are in control.

Children's libraries contain several basic functional areas, or zones. The zones differ in sizes, scales, and relationships, depending on the children's needs:

- Active area for toddlers and very young children with floor tables, cushions, colorful picture books, low tables and chairs, and some room for young children to move around easily
- Quiet refuge from noise and activity
- Space for parents and caregivers, who need to keep an eye on the young children
- Study area for older children, very distinct in design and location from the younger children's area (featuring electronic workstations, several ranges of book stacks, display shelving for books and media, study tables, carrels for individual study, and a group study area)
- Service desk with computers and reference materials for staff to use (may have checkout machines in addition to self-service checkout machines nearby)
- Staff work room for program and display preparation and material selection and storage
- Multipurpose program room with area for craft programs, storage for stacking chairs, and a sink

Designing for Children

Displays

To capture the attention of children coming into the library for the first time, place carefully selected, beautifully illustrated books in a spotlighted display area at the entrance. This area may also include:

- A flat screen programmable display for events
- Picture rails for art and a rack for hanging maps
- Seasonal decorations
- Tackable display walls

It is easy to make the mistake of overdecorating. Focus on a few relevant displays that will resonate with the season or with library events, and be certain to change displays frequently.

According to Paco Underhill (1999: 76), "When people enter a store they head rightward." Accordingly, major bookstores place their most attractive browsing sections to the right. Children's librarians should display their most attractive new materials to the right of the entrance.

Service Desk

If the service desk is located to the left of the entrance, then it will be on the right as people exit from the area. The location of the service desk may vary depending on the size of the area, other functions that take place at the desk, and its proximity to the exit of the library building. In larger libraries the customer service desk may be centrally located. In very small libraries there may be only a single service desk for both children and adults.

Creative Options—Themes and Imagination

To attract children, children's facilities are often designed with playful themes (see, e.g., Figure 4-1), such as houses, farms, stores, or kitchens. However, libraries are special places in themselves. Books, videos, music, images, and words encourage children's imagination. These items themselves should decorate the children's room. If themes are used, they should be related to books or other library activities and materials.

Images should flow naturally from the library's function to stimulate the imagination and to offer children a variety of materials and ways to experience these materials. Explicit themes may be of interest during the first visit, but they become stale and boring on repeated exposure and have little relevance to the imaginative world that library books create. It may be better to create frequently changing, interactive learning experiences with a variety of exhibits mounted on mobile carts or fitting right into bookshelves.

Books themselves should be the theme of the children's library. Authors' pictures, oversized books, and flat screen monitors featuring book characters can be more exciting than permanent wall murals, big stuffed animals, or fish tanks. Posters with large letters and varied calligraphy can also intrigue a child.

Figure 4-1
A reading area under a tree at the Wallingford (CT) Public Library,
designed by Bruce Tuthill.

Flexibility and Mobile Furnishings

The percentage of young children in a community will vary widely and will change over time. Zone requirements may also change as percentages of children in varied age groups change. Therefore, flexibility in the location of furniture and equipment will be vital. Ideally children's areas should be redesigned every five years in light of changing population, library roles, and mission.

Flexibility may be achieved by incorporating the following:

- Low shelving on Darnell-Rose ball-bearing casters and sled-based chairs or chairs on casters that will glide easily (children may occasionally play bumper chairs, but the need for flexibility outweighs occasional discipline problems)
- Wheelbarrow carrels with two wheels and two legs, allowing rapid relocation while retaining some stability
- Electrical and low-voltage receptacles distributed throughout the area, with plugs (containing childproof guards) at 36 inches above the floor
- Light fixture locations designed for task flexibility
- Acoustical partitions and sound-dampening materials
- Minimal fixed walls (use book stacks to separate zones)

Other Desirable Features

In colder climates, place coat racks for children near the program area as well as throughout the room for convenient access. Provide bicycle racks and stroller space outside near the entrance to the library, and protect them from the rain and snow.

Stroller space is an issue throughout the children's area. Standard 36-inch book stack aisle widths are minimal to accommodate strollers in stacks; wider 48-inch aisles would be better. Design program zones to allow stroller maneuverability.

Family care bathrooms and nursing zones are other features to consider. Family bathrooms allow caregivers, particularly men, to attend directly to children's needs. They should be large and may be more secure without doors so that sounds can be heard by staff. Nursing zones need to offer privacy and security by being clearly marked for private use only.

Specific Considerations to Enhance the Library Experience

How can design enhance the library experience for children, parents, caregivers, and staff? The following discussion provides specific ideas as they relate to the varied functions and zones dedicated to children.

Creating a Special Place for Children

Children should experience the library as an interesting, exciting, and calming place where they can listen to stories, look at puppet shows, browse with a parent, get help from a librarian, conduct research on the Internet, or download favorite music or programs.

Design considerations: Provide different-sized tables and chairs (including chairs large enough for a parent and child to sit together to read a book), open activity areas, and quiet study locations. Picture books, with their thin spines, tiny spine lettering, and large colorful covers, need special shelving treatment for easy browsing by children and parents.

Locating the Children's Area

Children and their parents and caregivers should be able to easily find the children's section from the library entrance. Parents will often be juggling their materials, one or more children, a stroller, and sometimes a wheelchair.

Design requirements: If the children's library is on the entry floor, it should be visible from the library entrance and indicated by the type and size of furnishings and/or decorations. If it is on another floor, signage indicating where the children's library is located should be in the direct line of sight of the entrance. Both stairs and elevator should be visible from the entrance. Automatic operating doors are a necessity for parents and caregivers with strollers.

Providing an Exciting, Resource-Rich Environment

Material displays should emulate those in a good bookstore. From my experience, books, DVDs, and CDs in an attractive display (like that shown in Figure 4-2) with covers well lighted for easy browsing create a welcoming environment.

Design requirements: Colorful covers brightly spotlighted and ever changing offer children exciting choices everywhere they look. For slanted, lighted displayers, no shelves should be lower than 12 inches or higher than 54 inches. Aisles should be 48 inches wide.

Figure 4-2
An attractive display of CD covers using the Lift Displayer, at East Longmeadow (MA) Public Library, designed by Stuart Roberts of Somerville, MA.

Offering Choices

The wide variety of services and activities require an understanding of how these functions relate to one another and how users find and use these functions.

Design considerations: Orientation for users and staff requires an intricate combination of signs, lighting, furnishings, zoning, and boundaries. To suggest opportunities for alternative behaviors, provide an open area for play and conversation and acoustically separated group and individual study areas.

Making It Easy to Find a Book

Librarians help people find just the right book, but children should also be able to find books on their own. Collections need to be uniformly arranged in an easy-to-find sequence. This is a special problem in children's libraries because there are separate sequences for different age levels and special topics such as science project books. A particular subject may be in several different locations.

Design considerations: Identify separate collections for easy finding using section and ceiling-mounted signs as well as shelf labels. Use large blocks (shown in Figure 4-3) and line-of-sight signage (shown in Figure 4-4) to signal topical or alphabetical sections. (Chapter 6 provides further suggestions on how to use graphics effectively.) Stack ranges that run at right angles to one another may be confusing.

The following visual aids make it easier for children to find books:

- End panel signs that guide children to the appropriate stack aisle
- Line-of-sight signage in aisles lighted for easy access to a particular subject
- Online public access computers mounted on end panels or distributed in the stacks
- Color-coding of shelf sections for Fiction and Nonfiction
- Different heights for Fiction and Nonfiction stacks
- Labels like "Stories" and "Information" rather than "Fiction" and "Nonfiction"

Decoding Dewey

Presenting the Dewey Decimal System as an interesting code to decipher may capture children's imagination, enticing them to see it as a magical way to classify and relate subjects. It helps children to understand relationships among subjects when they are organized according to a systematic and related numeric pattern.

The Dewey Decimal System has many virtues, unlike bar codes:

- It is universal. It is used in public libraries all over the world. Once you learn the subject that a number represents, the same number will always have the same meaning. Numbers are language independent; they represent the same subject in both English and non-English languages.
- The numbers organize all of the categories of all recorded knowledge into one system.
- The system progresses from general subjects (beginning with 000) to more specific subjects (ending with 999).
- Numbers show relationships.

Figure 4-3
Letter divider boxes at an English library help children find books.

Figure 4-4
Line-of-sight signage (by Brodart) is another way to help children find books.

- The initial number indicates the broad topic, while later numbers are specific. For example, 8 represents literature, 810 represents American literature, and 811 represents American poetry.

Design considerations: Children need to learn that Dewey Decimal numbers signify topics they will be studying in the future. Incorporate large Dewey numbers into exhibits related to the subjects. The most important factor in design is linking Dewey numbers to their subjects. Every time a number is shown it *must* be linked to its subject.

Ensuring a Place for Quiet Study

Children need a quiet place in the library to read a book, study reference material, or search databases or the Internet (see, e.g., Figure 4-5).

Design considerations: Provide acoustically separated and comfortable study locations with glare-free lighting and data transmission capabilities. Choose ergonomically designed, long-term, and mobile seating. Consider alcoves with seating surrounded by books.

Guiding Reading and Homework Choices

Experienced, knowledgeable librarians talk with children about their reading and help them to select books that meet their needs. They give homework assistance and help with searching the Internet.

Design considerations: Locate the staff service desk in a prominent place, and make sure it is well lighted and easily identified. Distribute smaller service stations throughout, and equip roaming staff with Vocera devices for quick communication. Place oversized collaborative electronic workstations, 48 inches wide with two chairs, within easy reach of a staff member.

Providing a Meeting Place

The library offers children and their parents and caregivers meeting spaces for small groups and large programs. Spaces designed for casual meetings, where parents and caregivers can share information yet keep an eye on their children, may make the library as popular as a local Starbucks.

Design requirements: The program area needs a sound system, equipment for video and electronic projection, and comfortable chairs. Ideally, the room will be available when the rest of the library is closed, and it will have extra space for food service and storage. Locate restrooms nearby.

Provide a variety of smaller, more intimate spaces for children, parents, and caregivers. Encourage casual meetings by appropriate arrangement of lounge seating, tables, and chairs. Choose laptop computers and other electronic devices that can be arranged and rearranged according to the needs of the group.

Providing a Comfortable Workplace

The activities of the library staff include the following:

- Assist children and caregivers in selecting useful materials
- Assist in searching the Internet
- Efficiently check out materials
- Prepare programs
- Select materials

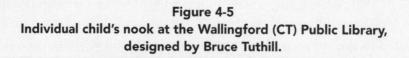

Figure 4-5
Individual child's nook at the Wallingford (CT) Public Library,
designed by Bruce Tuthill.

Design requirements: Make sure that sight lines are clear. Locate the service desk close to the exit and to work and storage spaces. Children's room staff need lots of storage space because they are frequently involved in creating exhibits and programs. Seasonal programs must also be stored from year to year.

Children Differ from Adults in How They Use the Library

The First Experience

As the saying goes, "There is never a second chance to make a first impression." It is crucial that children's first experiences in a library be rewarding. When they come for the first time, children will need assistance and encouragement to become comfortable in a totally new environment.

Variations in Size

Children vary greatly in size. Therefore, chairs, tables, and book stack heights of all sizes are needed. Toilet fixtures and drinking fountains also need to be varied.

Variations in Vocabulary

Children of different ages will vary in their ability to comprehend reading materials, so there needs to be a variety of sequences of materials arranged by vocabulary level. Children's reading abilities are also influenced by their socioeconomic background and by the presence or absence of a reading disability. By making a variety of levels of material available, all children should be able to find something that suits their level.

Selection by Front Cover in Addition to Subject, Title, or Author

Children who do not know how to read often select materials by their covers. Put picture books with colorful covers in bins so that children can select a book based on the cover. Insert alphabetic dividers with large letters to sequence the books. Although bins may reduce the capacity to store materials, the increased circulation of materials will help compensate. The goal is to encourage use, so bins are better than other types of shelving for younger children who can't read the tiny spine labels but will be attracted to the colorful covers.

Variations in Activity Level

Children change quickly between their need for activity and their need for quiet. Therefore, provide sufficient room to roam around in as well as shelter and quiet. Place the active and quiet zones physically close together with clear visibility between the two. The child who is active one moment may the next moment suddenly wander away looking for a place to curl up for a nap, and parents and caregivers need to know when this happens.

Increased Need for Staff Attention

Children need more staff assistance than most adults to learn how to use the library. Librarians encourage children to read by helping them find just the right book.

Self-Service and Staff Service

Children's facilities give librarians opportunities to help children as well as guiding children to help themselves. Parents and caregivers ask librarians to help them find specific books for their children, but children love to find books by themselves.

Librarians work with children and their caregivers to transfer knowledge and skills in finding materials. Children, especially toddlers, need to be able to select books by looking at the beautifully designed front covers, while librarians and caregivers need to be able to find an age-appropriate book or a topic by having collections arranged in an orderly sequential fashion on the shelves.

- The bottom shelf is easy for children to reach, while higher shelves are much more convenient for adults.
- Children want both cozy, small-scale spaces and room to roam around, while librarians and caregivers want to be able to keep an eye on the children at all times.

Security and Safety

Child safety is a major concern in our security-conscious society. Children need to be closely monitored by staff for safety and security reasons. Staff as well as parents and caregivers need to know where children are at all times. Therefore, security and safety concerns often dictate design.

Keeping children in their own part of the library where caregivers and staff can see them is a major design objective. It is especially important to keep children from running out of the first floor of a building and into automobile traffic or from escaping down a staircase or an elevator.

For safety, use triple-padded carpeting where there are raised areas in the room from which children might fall. No furniture should have sharp corners.

Bathrooms provide special concerns and need to be located close to staff areas for surveillance. Doorless bathrooms such as those found in airports make audio surveillance easier. Children entering bathrooms that can be locked or that conceal sounds with doors may make children more vulnerable.

Chapter Summary

This chapter begins with showing how conflicting objectives in design require thoughtful responses. It then discusses convenient use and efficient staff operation, including the following:

- Movable furnishings are necessary.
- Functional subdivisions respond to the variety of library users and their differing needs.
- Children's libraries are resource-rich environments that must respond to different levels of need and ability.
- Children and adult libraries differ because of user size, experience differences, and variations in vocabulary.
- Staff must be able to help children easily, but children should also be able to help themselves.
- Dividing the library into age and user zones can be accomplished by a variety of techniques.

Reference

Underhill, Paco. 1999. *Why We Buy*. New York: Simon & Schuster.

5

Organizing the Children's Area

This chapter begins with a discussion of organic design and spatial relationships. Next, the chapter moves on to shapes and zoning considerations. Then, different functions within the library are put into context by the library's various users to provide the best ideas for organization of the children's area.

Organic Design

Libraries are organic buildings, ever growing and changing. The design should be flexible to accommodate change.

Keep vertical access elements to the perimeter of the structure to ensure future functional flexibility. These elements include elevators, stairways, heating and air-conditioning ducts, and electrical risers.

Include a master plan in the initial stages of planning to accommodate change and growth both within and in addition to the building being constructed at this time. For example, show specific areas designated to accommodate future expansion in collections, seating, and multipurpose space.

Discuss internal change scenarios, such as the change from material storage to computer workstations. Short-term, five-year changes are more useful than speculative, longer-term plans. Include furniture and equipment sketches as well as footprint site expansion diagrams.

Wiring for computers requires both power distribution and low-voltage transmission features such as telephone lines. Run them in separate conduits, which should be easily accessible for increasing bandwidth when needed. Improved bandwidth delivery systems may require rewiring during the life of the building, so design electronic equipment centers and conduits for ease of rewiring.

Computer workstations should be capable of easy movement throughout the facility. Discuss such options as wireless, fiber-optic cabling, carpet tile/flat wiring, power poles, Walkerducts, and floor grids for power early in the planning stage. Wireless systems provide a useful option for new and old installations. Conduct a wireless evaluation to determine suitability and plan for future hubs.

Identify special electrical and communication centers early in the planning process to ensure sufficient power both overall and per circuit. A well-designed power center design will include dedicated circuits; telephone transmission options; filtered, uniform, and stable power delivery; ease of equipment exchange for repair; and ease of access to clearly labeled circuit breakers. These special centers will be located throughout the library, including the following places:

- Checkout stations
- Staff work areas
- Multipurpose and meeting rooms
- Security stations
- Electronic networking centers

Design spaces to accommodate multiple purposes. The computer instruction area should be flexibly designed so that individuals can use the electronic workstations when classes are not in session. The story and crafts area should be carefully designed for three very different functions:

- Storyhours, which require that children be able to concentrate on the storyteller with sound separation from other library functions
- Dramatizations, such as puppet shows, with a stage, curtains, and spotlighting
- Crafts, which require a flooring material that can be easily cleaned and a sink

Future Furnishings

About 10 percent of the equipment may be purchased after the first year of occupancy in order to respond to the changing needs of library users. People will use a new facility differently, and it will take a year before their preferences will be realized.

The "flexibility fallacy" refers to the assumption that library functions are interchangeable and that particular functions do not have specific design requirements. Beware assuming that a uniform design allows for functional change without major alterations. For example, placing stacks in a high-ceiling area designed as a reading room requires lighting and heating, ventilation, and air-conditioning (HVAC) adjustments difficult to achieve and may look ugly. Electronic workstations in a former stack may not have adequate HVAC or lighting.

Spatial Relationships and Traffic Flow

The design must make it easy for children to find and use materials and services. It must be clear and logical to all, including first-time children and adult visitors. People entering the children's area may be pushing strollers and may have their hands full of materials, so wide automatic doors may be useful.

Library Service Choices and Traffic Flow

The entrance to the children's area should afford a clear view of the various age and activity subdivisions within the area. Younger children should be able to reach their part of the area without walking through the part of the room designed for older children to study. Older children and preteens should not have to walk through picture books and young children playing on the floor.

User Groups

Those who come to the library will usually fall into one of the groups described in this section. The building design must conveniently accommodate them all.

THE SHORT-TERM USER

Some users enter with the intention of making only a brief trip, often to return previously borrowed materials. Some wish to pick up reserved books or to get a quick answer. Others wish to quickly browse new books or skim magazines and newspapers. From one-third to one-half of the users fall into this category and stay 30 minutes or less.

THE LONG-TERM USER

The long-term user comes for extended periods of time to browse through collections, read magazines and newspapers, use materials in the library, search the Internet, or study. Students will come to study after school or on weekends. These individuals need a quiet environment for their activities. They would especially appreciate small, acoustically separated rooms for group study.

GROUP ACTIVITY PARTICIPANTS

Children and their parents and caregivers will come to the library to participate in particular activities or programs such as public lectures and toddler storyhours. Because groups can cause traffic problems and create congestion, noise, and confusion, access to meeting areas should be carefully planned to avoid routing through reading or stack areas.

CHILDREN WHO COME WITH CAREGIVERS

Young children will often work closely with their adult companions, so the library should provide larger, oversized chairs so that they can sit together. Parenting materials and adult books may also be needed near the young children's area. Caregivers may want to take the opportunity to talk with one another, and groupings of seats will accommodate this.

CHILDREN WHO COME ALONE

Although the children who come alone are often older children, they may still need a librarian's help in finding their way around the library. This is especially true for less experienced library users like younger children. Libraries try to be self-service institutions, with catalogs and signage to show people where things are and how they work. The wording of such signs should be understandable by children as well as adults. Signs using pictorial symbols and Dewey Decimal numbers to help children find their favorite subjects may be helpful in the book stacks.

Spatial Relationships to the Building Entrance

The building's entrance and lobby should be compact and free of visual obstructions for safety and security reasons. Sufficient room for traffic flow and potential conflicts in traffic patterns should be studied and designed for. Those entering and leaving the library or stopping to pick up brochures as well as others moving from one section to another can be a problem.

A key design challenge of the lobby is to seamlessly integrate a wide variety of services yet maintain acoustic separation and good visual control. The decor of the lobby should be friendly but organized and purposeful. The service desk and new materials should be visible. Visitors should be able to see where the many other library areas are located.

Children's areas located at street level are especially vulnerable to children wandering off by themselves. They need to have staff constantly monitoring the exits. Non-entry-level locations may require gates to prevent children from escaping onto stairways or elevators.

The location of children's rooms in relation to library entrances is often controversial. If they are on the main floor, children may exit the building quickly, but they don't have to contend with waiting for elevators or using stairs. If the children's room is on an upper floor, children are farther from the exit but must use stairs or an elevator to reach their location.

Organizing Functional Areas

Figures 5-1 through 5-3 show examples of how the major functional areas in a children's library can be arranged. They do not include all furniture and equipment, only seats and book stacks. Staff work areas are also not included, and the younger children's area picture books are in bins. Electronic workstations can be located at any of the seating areas, with wireless connection routers distributed throughout the library at sufficient intervals.

The Traditional Approach

Figure 5-1 shows a traditional layout for a library of approximately 3,000 square feet, appropriate for a small town with a population of about 15,000. The staff service desk is located near the entrance in an open area surrounded by the younger children's materials, picture books, board books, and easy readers. Parents might like to be near their younger children. Storyhour program space may also be located near the entrance for convenient immediate access without disturbing older children who are doing homework or studying.

Areas for the older children are located at the rear. Computers and seating areas are separated acoustically by book stacks or a glass partition from the younger children. A disadvantage of the traditional arrangement is that some older children who have to walk through the area designed for younger children may be discouraged from coming to the library.

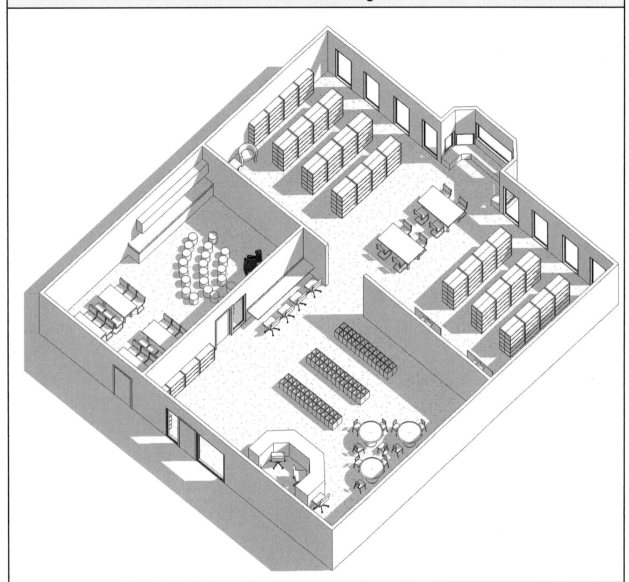

Figure 5-1
Traditional library layout (CAD drawing by Barbara Joslin of JCJ Architects). The entrance to the staff service desk and the younger children's area are on the right. The multipurpose program area entrance is on the left. The older children's reading area and book stacks are at the rear.

Centralized Staff Approach

Figure 5-2 presents a newer alternative plan for a larger children's facility located on one level. Figure 5-3 (see p. 68) shows the layout for the very large, two-story children's Library Discovery Center designed by Juergen Riehm of 1100 Architect in New York City.

According to the centralized staff approach, the staff service and work areas are located in the center of the children's room, which allows staff to be more readily accessible for a variety of activities and to multiple categories of users. Older children enter the area on the left, and younger children enter on the right. This alternative places staff further away from the entrance/exit of the area.

Figure 5-2
Centralized staff arrangement (drawing by Barbara Joslin of JCJ Architects).

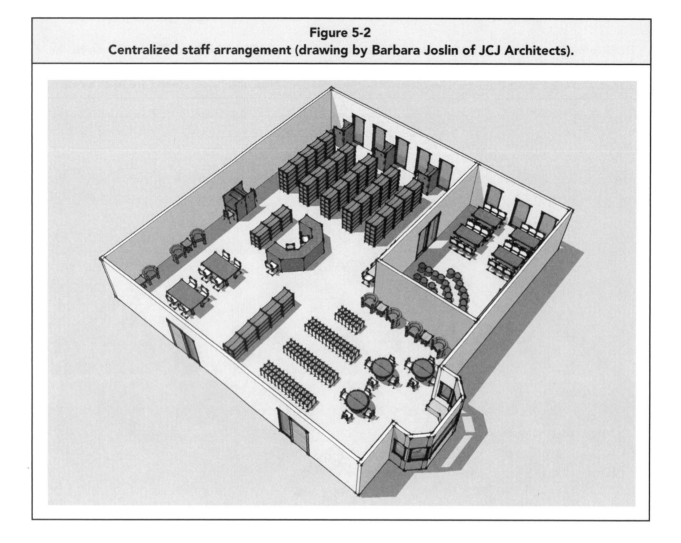

Locating storyhour programming space in the back of the children's room means that large audiences arriving at one time may disturb activities as they walk through the other parts of the room. However, once they get to the storyhour room, they and sounds from the program itself are less likely to interrupt the other library users.

Children coming to the library to do homework or study for longer periods of time may appreciate the opportunity to find a quiet, secluded part of the room. If separate study rooms cannot be provided, such areas can be created around the perimeter of the room. One benefit to this arrangement is that using the natural light from windows can help offset energy bills. Staff should always have a clear view of these study locations.

Rectangular versus Square Shape

The shape of the children's room can be rectangular or square. A square shape has the advantage of keeping activities closer to the center of the room, whereas in an elongated rectangular space some activities will be farther away. This problem may be alleviated by splitting the staff service and staff work areas so that librarians can monitor two different parts of the room. A minor disadvantage may be the difficulty for staff to move between the staff service area and the work area. An advantage, however, may be

Figure 5-3
Cutting-edge design for the two-story Children's Library Discovery Center, Queens, NY, created by Juergen Riehm of 1100 Architect; Peter Magnani, Director of Capital and Facilities Management; and Rene Tablante, New York City Department of Design and Construction. The top image shows the main floor entrance and the young children's area, which has Exploratorium exhibits. The bottom image shows the second floor, where the older children's area, staff work area, and program room are located.

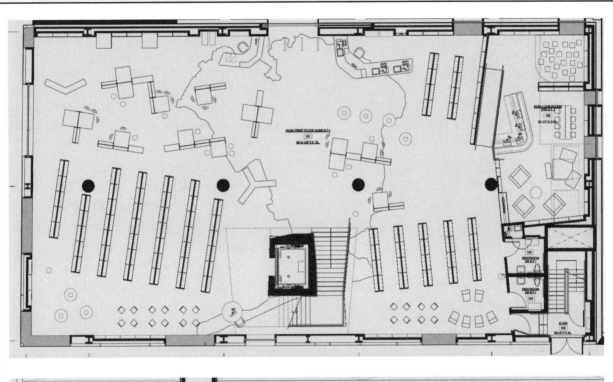

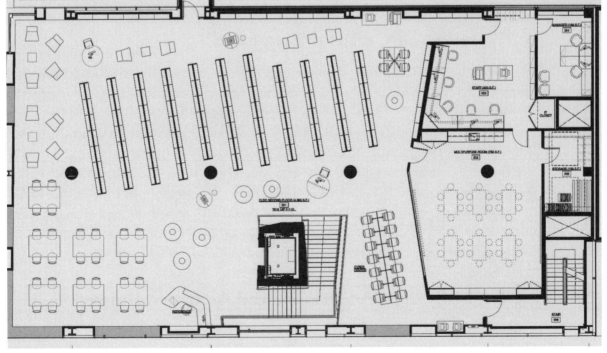

that they are less likely to be interrupted when working on behind-the-scenes preparation for storyhours or selecting books.

Handicapped Access

The U.S. Department of Justice requires that all new public and commercial building construction (and most renovation) designs incorporate features to make buildings comfortable and usable by people with physical disabilities. For libraries, handicapped children should be accommodated in the mainstream of the design rather than through special entrances or arrangements. According to the federal guidelines, as provided in *ADA Standards for Accessible Design* (www.ada.gov/adastd94.pdf):

- Interior and exterior ramps should have gentle slopes of 16 feet of horizontal travel for each foot of vertical rise. If ramps are over 30 feet long, then an even gentler slope of 1 in 20 feet is preferred. Minimum for short ramps is 1 in 12 feet.
- Aisle widths should be 3 feet minimum, but I recommend 4 feet.
- Service counters should be no more than 36 inches high.
- At least 5 percent of tables and carrels should accommodate wheelchairs with knee space 19 inches deep and 27 inches high from floor to underside of tables.
- Table skirts should have 26 inch knee clearance.
- At least one restroom facility must be handicap accessible.
- Reach height for magazines should be 48 inches maximum for front approach and 54 inches for side approach.

Section 8 of the *ADA Standards for Accessible Design* specifically addresses libraries. Numerous diagrams clearly show how to incorporate the specific dimensions into the overall design.

Diversity and Cultural Response

Libraries in the twenty-first century are evolving into multicultural institutions with several different language collections and a strong emphasis on language instruction. The library design should be sensitive to opportunities for responding to the cultural aesthetics of the populations to be served. Banners, colors, patterns, furniture types, and decorative touches can be attractive responses.

Beware, however, of rapidly changing demographics. An urban library recently selected German chair decorations and design for a branch library in a German neighborhood that rapidly became Puerto Rican. Avoid ethnic wall murals or major design elements that are difficult to change. The library's great virtue is that it is a place that celebrates diversity with constantly changing organic materials.

New Buildings, Additions, and Adaptive Reuse

Most architects and librarians would prefer to deal with a clean slate and design a brand-new library. There are clear advantages:

- Planning for new and future services is easier.
- Space for future growth can be included.
- The wiring system can be designed flexibly to handle future growth.
- Cost-effective staff adjacencies are not limited by an existing structure.
- All handicap accessibility requirements can be met.
- The library will have a unified design.
- Temporary relocation will not be needed to accommodate renovations.

There are also a few disadvantages:

- A new location may disorient some library users.
- A historic structure familiar to the community may be lost.
- New construction is more expensive.

Advantages and disadvantages to adding on to an existing building or renovating it include the following:

- Advantages
  - A known and familiar location and design can be retained.
  - Beautiful architectural detailing that may be difficult to reproduce can be saved.
  - It is usually less expensive to add or renovate than to begin from scratch.
- Disadvantages
  - Bringing an older building into compliance with modern safety codes can be expensive and time-consuming.
  - Temporary relocation may be necessary. Staying in a building while an addition is built is difficult because of the noisy, dusty renovation and construction activity.
  - Electrical, heating, air-conditioning, and ventilating systems will at times need to be shut down.
  - Vertical construction activity such as the installation of plumbing or electrical risers is disruptive.

Adaptive reuse of other building types, such as converting a shopping center or former school building to a library, presents interesting opportunities and problems:

- Advantages
  - Retail stores are often in excellent locations for attracting library users.
  - Shopping centers often have large parking lots and convenient automobile access to the entrance.
  - The cost of abandoned buildings is often quite low.
- Disadvantages
  - Schools are often located far from retail or downtown locations.
  - Floor load capacities for stores, offices, and schools are much lower than the 150 pounds per square foot live loads required for standard book stacks. Reinforcing floors is expensive and problematical.
  - Not all existing buildings can be made handicap accessible.

One-Story versus Multistory Libraries

Very few children's libraries serve such large populations that multiple floors are needed. In large libraries, placing young children on one level and older children and preteens on another has the advantage of separating noisy younger children from quieter purposeful older children. However, it may result in staff inefficiencies and is difficult for older children who are caregivers to younger siblings. If one floor has more activity than the other floor, staff may not be able to assist one another as easily as if they were all on one floor.

When a new library is being planned, the decision will have to be made whether it will be a one-story or taller building. One-story libraries are preferred.

One-story libraries provide maximum and universal access to all materials. All materials will be equally accessible if they are all on one level. Those materials on a level above or below the entry level will be less used because more effort is required to find them.

Services on one level will enhance public convenience. When all services can be seen from the entrance, the public will be aware of the clear choices of activities. The public is often unaware of services on other levels.

Staff can be more productive in one-level facilities. Adding a single professional staff member will cost the library $1 million over the 20-year life of the building. In a one-level library, staff can be involved in a variety of public services as they are needed rather than having main floor staff be busy while second floor staff are idle. Experienced staff can assist newer staff better if they work in close proximity.

One-story buildings are generally less expensive to construct than taller ones. Elevators are costly to install and maintain, and they deny access to other floors when they are broken. Staff and users also lose time by having to wait for them. Libraries are often open many hours a week, requiring two shifts. Staffing two or more levels on a two-shift basis greatly increases operating costs.

Security of staff, public, and materials is easier to ensure in a one-story facility because all activities are visible from a central service area. One security disadvantage is the possibility of children wandering out of the building. If the library has two floors, the children's services can be located on the second floor, making it harder for children to leave the building unseen, but the children then need to use stairs or an elevator to reach their area.

Some services are more amenable than others to being located on a level other than the main floor, although they will require some additional cost in staff and supervision. If the children's services are on the second floor, then program, multipurpose, and meeting rooms should also be on the second floor. Parents and caregivers will not have to make special trips throughout the building to check out books and attend storyhours during the same visit. Staff work areas can be located on another floor; however, restricted communication and movement between levels may hinder productivity, and public service staff will not be easily available to assist children at public service stations. Computer and learning labs can also be located on another floor.

Zones and Boundaries

In older libraries, the different library functions are often separated by solid walls. Architects understood that libraries required different activities that needed to be expressed in the design. Accordingly, library book stacks were often placed in spaces with low ceilings and lighting only on the books. Separate reading rooms, on the other hand, had high ceilings with tall windows carefully spaced to allow natural light to pour onto the reading tables. These separate spaces were inflexible and difficult to access when the reading room and book stacks were not located on the same floors.

Flexible, open-plan libraries use different ways to separate different functions. Zones and boundaries separate activities that can conflict with one another, such as the following:

- Activities designed for specific age groups, such as young adults and preschoolers
- Displays featuring new materials, which are used more often than older materials
- Programs and meetings
- Staff processing, ordering, and maintenance activities

Changes in functions within libraries require several flexible methods to express functional zones and boundaries:

- Furniture types and sizes differ according to function, such as widely spaced individual study tables for quiet study and sofas, lounge seats, and group study tables for noisier group or conversational activities.
- Bright colors can indicate noisy children's activity areas, and natural, subdued colors are used in study areas.
- Bright spotlighting indicates bustling display spaces, and indirect low lighting indicates quieter spaces.
- Low partitions in the children's room set apart active from quieter areas.
- Glass partitions separate areas acoustically while allowing visual access. Glass on all four sides of an area produces echo noise, so acoustical glass should be used. Lighting that washes the face of the glass reduces reflections.
- Varied ceiling heights created by suspended ceilings can indicate different activities.
- Lower or higher book stacks and wider aisle spacing differentiate active display areas from the less used book storage stacks.
- Vertical separation of areas by a low step and ramp can differentiate functions (ramps need to be 1 foot long for every 1 inch of height).
- Book stacks are useful in absorbing sound and defining boundaries.
- Graphics, especially backlighted signs, are an excellent method of signaling and defining important staff service points.
- Passageways separate functions by not having any furniture.
- Carpet color and pattern variations can differentiate function while facilitating recarpeting of more active areas.

Activities that produce different levels of noise, such as listening, viewing, reading, and studying in groups, have correspondingly different zoning requirements. The following techniques can help control noise:

- Enclose the area, still the most effective method of isolating noisy or quiet activities.
- Use sound-absorbing construction materials, such as acoustical tiles, anechoic foam wedges, or perforated metal screens. Note that books are also excellent at absorbing sound, whereas glass reflects sound and results in echoes.
- Switch to carpets, cork floors, and upholstered furniture.
- Apply the concept of "distance." Noise decreases greatly with distance.
- Selectively supply white sound to mask out unwanted noise.

Rhythm of Use

During the morning hours, users often include very young children and preschool groups. Young users need more guidance than older children, who are often more experienced at how the library works. Younger users also need to be carefully monitored for safety and security reasons. Caregivers are also present, and they may want to visit with one another and chat in addition to using library services.

After school hours, older children will come to the library alone or in small groups. They are generally knowledgeable about how the library works and therefore do not need as much staff guidance. On the other hand, they may be noisy and boisterous after being cooped up in school all day.

Parents and grandparents are more likely to come to the library during evening hours and holidays. More people will also be present in the periods both before and after programs, requiring more staff attention.

Chapter Summary

This chapter on organizing space emphasizes the organic nature of children's services. The flexible design response should take into account age and activity differences as well as staff needs. New buildings, additions, and adaptive reuse are compared, and cultural diversity and handicapped requirements are outlined. The use of the children's library will differ depending on the time of the day and the day of the week. The following summarizes children's needs and appropriate design responses:

Needs	Design Responses
Changing behaviors	Alternate noisy and quiet areas
Having active fun	Provide open space
Finding things	Explain sequenced materials, Dewey Decimal numbers, and subjects with signage
Refuge	Create quiet, contained, sheltered spaces
Varying functions	Install flexible, mobile furnishings on wheels
Changing sizes	Provide different-sized chairs and tables
Group study	Create small, acoustically dampened or separated study areas

6

Entrances, Displays, Graphics, and Lighting

This chapter discusses how the entrance can be both interesting and informative in explaining how a library works. As a child moves from the entrance into the children's area, it is important to encounter a welcoming open space accompanied by quiet, cozy areas. At and beyond the entrance, displays, graphics, and lighting work together to make the library easier to use and to create an interesting and welcoming variety of spaces.

Entrances

An entry to the children's area can be defined by supergraphics, as in the Robin Hood Libraries described in Chapter 1 (see Figures 6-1 and 6-2). Often colors and furnishings will be sufficient to define the space. Changes in ceiling height are also used, and some libraries have special low entry doors for children, though this may be inconvenient for adults, who will need to use a separate entrance. I have fantasized that an interesting way to enter a children's library might be down a slide.

When the doors open, children's eyes will scan the surrounding area, looking for something that interests them. This is where the combination of displays, graphics, and lighting can help enhance the entrance experience.

Displays

Use displays to help capture children's attention upon entering the library. Highlight varieties of materials in the children's library in a special display in the entrance. Show front book covers and audiovisual jackets rather than stacked spines (see Figure 6-3, p. 76).

Create a second display in the entrance featuring library events for parents and children. A flat-screen programmable display is useful for this purpose. The display might also include samples of children's art produced during past events.

Provide a clearly organized orienting view of other children's service areas. One method to enhance orientation is to create a color-coded directory and signage system. The sections listed on the directory are identified throughout by signs of the same color. For example, "Reference Section" is written in orange on the directory, and all

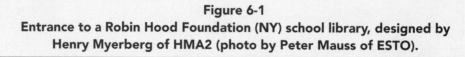

Figure 6-1
Entrance to a Robin Hood Foundation (NY) school library, designed by
Henry Myerberg of HMA2 (photo by Peter Mauss of ESTO).

signs throughout the library that indicate where the Reference Section is are in the
same shade of orange.

Changeable displays and seasonal decorations are an important aspect of the children's area. Tackable display walls and display cases located strategically throughout
the area are useful for temporary displays. Drawings, photographs, poems, and pieces
of art from past programs are effective in these types of displays too.

Beyond the entrance, displays can be used to control spatial densities and degrees
of openness. The need to monitor children can conflict with the child's need for privacy.
Research into design options has produced somewhat contradictory and ambiguous
results. Studies have shown that spatial density tends to increase aggression among
preschool children. At the same time, open areas tend to result in running and cross-
room talking. Activity areas with partitions tend to increase cooperative behavior. The
answer may be to use displays as low dividers between activity areas. Taller displays

Figure 6-2
Poetry adorning the walls beyond the entrance to a Robin Hood Foundation (NY) school library, designed by Henry Myerberg of HMA2 (photo by Peter Mauss of ESTO).

can be used as space dividers for older children. Furnishings and displays should always be low enough so that children can see and be seen by staff.

Children may seek relief in quiet alcoves away from overactive open areas. Creating a cozy, comfortable corner is often mentioned in staff objectives for children's design.

Graphics and Wayfinding

A library is often a self-service operation, but the wide variety of services and materials offered by libraries require explanation and guidance. Signs help users find their way to a particular book with minimal staff assistance. Lighting, furnishings, and colors work together with graphics to assist children, parents, and caregivers in differentiating among services. For graphics to work effectively, they must be planned early in the design to coordinate with interior design color schemes and especially lighting.

Figure 6-3
Media bins by Bibliomodell, designed by Michael Cohen of FHCM of Boston, MA.

The following guidelines are helpful in producing effective graphics:

- Post library hours at the entrance, directly in the line of sight of people entering the area. When appropriate, also post exceptions to these hours, such as special holiday schedules.
- When selecting text sizes, consider distance. One-inch-high letters are suitable for 50 feet of visibility. For every additional 50 feet of visibility desired, increase the text size 1 inch. Therefore, 2-inch-high letters are needed for a sign designed to be seen 100 feet away.
- When selecting text colors, consider background. A dark background sign with white or light-colored letters is easier to read than the reverse and avoids the glare reflected from a light background.
- Use a simple, direct, familiar type style that is easily obtainable and easy to read, such as Helvetica.
- Graphics can be aesthetically pleasing as well as functional, and they should be designed to coordinate with the architecture and furnishings.
- Coordinate location, colors, furnishings, lightings, and graphics at an early planning stage, not after construction is completed.
- Avoid negative signs, especially large permanent ones that are difficult to enforce, such as "No food in the library."
- Fliers, posters, maps, and directories may be more useful than signs.
- The standard height center point is 54 inches.
- Use capitals and lowercase letters rather than all capitals.

- Never stack letters one on top of the other in this way:

  B
  O
  O
  K
  S

- When using both arrows and text to indicate directions, use separate panels for each so that text can be changed without having to change the arrows.
- Make sure exterior signs are lighted, include hours open, and are placed perpendicular to traffic. Signs intended to be noticed by people in cars will have to be larger than those designed for pedestrians. Outdoor signs are useful reminders of a library's availability, not just its location.
- Identify user categories, such as Teenagers or Toddlers, and chart the paths to these destinations in preparation for specifications. Plan by:
  - User category
  - User destination
  - Traffic flow
  - Decision points where patrons pause or turn
- Place signs above the desks. Signs located on the front of busy counters, such as the circulation or reference desks, are invisible when library patrons are standing there.
- Use ADA requirements for type and placement of signs.
- Use line-of-sight signage in book stacks that project into the aisle (see Figure 6-4). This makes it easier to see the major Dewey numbers and subject divisions from a distance.

Lighting

Louis Kahn, one of the greatest of modern architects, wrote in his program for the Phillips Exeter school library in New Hampshire that "libraries are about books, people and light." How the library is lighted can make the difference between a bland, gray, industrial look and an exciting, glorious space in which the materials become the decoration and people have a marvelous choice of sunlit reading and study spaces and cozy, comfortable individual study carrels.

The rest of the chapter provides useful ideas and information about lighting that will help designers create a beautiful and functional library.

Controlling Sunlight

Be careful of direct sunlight. Weather changes make it unpredictable and difficult to count on. Ultraviolet light from the sun damages paper, bindings, and ink. Use overhangs and awnings to control direct sunlight. New products, such as high-E windows and fritted glass, now filter sunlight and reduce the heat gain that formerly made perimeter window seats unusable on hot summer days.

Indirect natural sunlight is wonderful for library users and should be introduced into all library areas except, perhaps, the program rooms. Consider clerestory windows set

Figure 6-4
Line-of-sight signage (by Brodart).

back from the sidewalls to bring natural indirect light into the middle of the library. On the top floor, roof monitors may also be useful in bringing natural light into the interior.

Controlling Glare

In many libraries designed before energy conservation became a concern, large numbers of fluorescent lamps were placed in the ceilings to mimic the effect of skylights. However, people using these libraries suffered from glare, which often produced headaches.

Select lenses for light fixtures that will diffuse light and prevent glare. These can be simple egg crate lenses (composed of small squares of plastic) or more directional parabolic units.

Parawedge louvers minimize ceiling brightness and ceiling reflections but provide very directional lighting, and they do not eliminate direct glare. They come in many sizes. The larger 2-inch-square louvers are not as useful in limiting glare as the smaller 1-inch-square ones.

Indirect Lighting and Spotlighting

With the advent of low-energy-consuming, high-intensity discharge lamps, lighting engineers began to recommend indirect lighting, using the ceiling to reflect and diffuse uniform high levels of light. By reflecting the light from the ceiling, the light rays strike the reading surfaces from many directions, which all but eliminates glare. However, the brightly lighted ceiling contrasts with the relatively dark furnishings and books.

The uniform diffused light produces a bland and dull effect on the materials and furnishings. Effective indirect lighting depends on the color and distance of the ceiling from the light source as well as the brightness of the lamps.

In areas of the library where a variety of tasks are performed in close proximity, use a system that will deliver uniform indirect light over the entire area. Install indirect lighting fixtures under a white reflective ceiling so that the light will shine up and be diffused by the ceiling over a wide area. This indirect light strikes the viewing surfaces from many angles, thus diffusing glare and providing a comfortable reading level for most tasks.

If the light source is hidden from view there will be no glare from the light to disturb long-term users. This follows Frank Lloyd Wright's dictum "Hide the lumenaires." Computer screens will also be protected from annoying reflections. An excellent example of this type of indirect lighting is the computer room in the Science Industry and Business Branch of the New York Public Library at 42nd Street and Madison Avenue in New York. The disadvantage of this indirect system is that the ceiling becomes the brightest object in the room, and the rest of the room may be darker and less interesting as a result.

Spotlighting of exhibits of interesting books throughout the library will add to the color and interest of the browsing experience. In the browsing area, where the front covers of books, DVDs, videos, and CDs are featured, it is advisable to supplement the indirect light with dramatic spotlighting as in bookstore displays (see Figure 6-5).

There are several types of lamps to choose from:

- Fluorescent lamps provide high light output for low cost, burn for over 10,000 hours, and come in a variety of colors.
- High-intensity discharge lamps provide even higher light output than fluorescent and an equal lamp life, but they come in fewer colors.
- Incandescent lamps burn for less than a 1,000 hours and provide lower light output than the other two types. These can be used for spot or flood lamps. They burn hot, resulting in heat gain. The lamps should be well ventilated for longer lamp life.
- Compact fluorescent and halogen lamps save power and last longer.

New fluorescent lamps such as the Ott light provide healthier, full-spectrum light that is similar to sunlight. The color of light from warm white fluorescent lamps (not deluxe) provides a better rendition of skin tones than cool white lamps. A color rendering index (CRI) of 75 is preferred.

Book Stack Lighting

It is possible to light book stacks indirectly. However, the narrow book spines and small type are often difficult to see in dim, indirect light.

Direct lighting of book stacks with fixtures that run parallel to the stack ranges and are hung from the ceiling will dramatize the materials and may result in more use of materials. A recently introduced 30/30 stack light designed by Sylvan Shemitz of New Haven (available from www.elliptipar.com) delivers 30 foot-candles of illumination measured vertically 30 inches from the floor and meets the California energy consumption standards of a maximum of 1.5 watts per square foot of space (see Figure 6-6).

Figure 6-5
New individual shelf lighting from LucaLight (www.insidedisplay.com).

Energy Consumption and Operating Cost

Ease of maintenance, replacement, and fixture cleaning are important for extending the life of the lighting system. Energy efficiency (electronic ballasts), life of lamps, and initial and replacement cost should be considered when selecting and locating fixtures.

Select fixtures, lenses, and lamps that are easy to clean and replace and that burn cool. Use low-intensity light in nonreading areas, such as traffic aisles. Control glare and reflection by diffusers, louvers, and light locations. Let users control task lighting. Use table and floor lamps.

White ceilings and white walls will increase light, especially in small rooms. Limit light intensity variation in small rooms or in contiguous areas.

Light-colored reflective floor materials increase light on the bottom shelves more than carpeting. Cork floors are reflective and absorb sound.

Visibility

Visibility in a room is affected by the size of the room, colors and contrasts within the room, as well as the brightness of lamps. Select incandescent lamps for concentration (very narrow spots) or spreading of light (flood lamps) and for color rendition.

Locate fixtures to minimize ceiling brightness and ceiling reflectance caused by light striking the viewing surface at a 45-degree angle. This is especially important in computer areas.

Light fixture locations must be coordinated with location of graphics to ensure that light does not obscure the signs. This can be achieved only by planning graphics and lighting at the same time during the project. Too often graphics planning is done too late to coordinate with lighting.

Layered Lighting

Layered lighting combines ambient and task lighting:

Figure 6-6
New 30/30 Stack Light, designed by Sy Shemitz of Elliptipar, New Haven, CT (www.elliptipar.com).

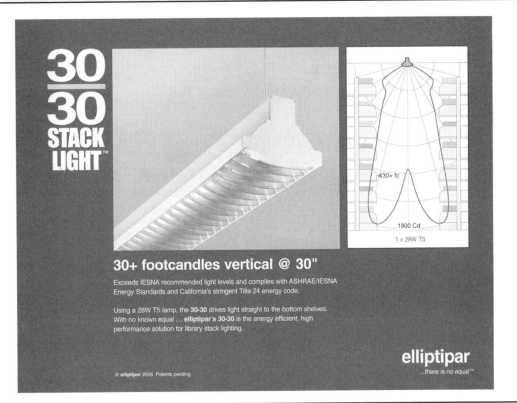

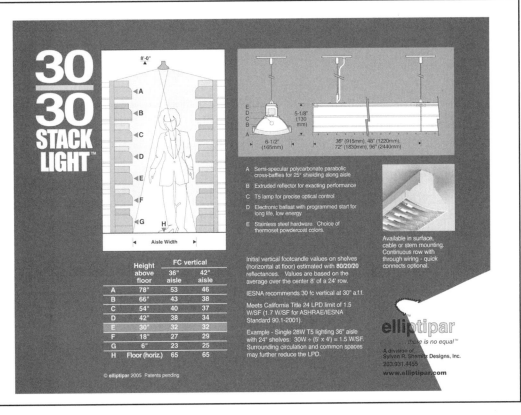

- Ambient lighting: A low level of ambient lighting will provide for general illumination. This ambient lighting will be low glare and accomplished by perimeter lighting units as well as hanging lamps that indirectly reflect light from a white ceiling.
- Task lighting: Nonglare task lighting will be directly related to functions such as illumination of displays, reading surfaces, and lounge seating. Task lighting can be provided by floor or table lamps or by recessed ceiling fixtures. Task lighting should be as adjustable as possible, including long, flexible electrical wires attached to ceiling fixtures, so that they may be easily relocated when functions change. Users should be able to control the task lighting, for example, with lamps on swivel arms.

Wall Wash Display Lighting

Perimeter, ceiling-mounted wall wash book display lighting fixtures should be installed at least 3 feet out from the walls and include elliptical reflectors in order to cast light all the way down the wall. The elliptipar fixture (available from www.elliptipar.com) is ideal for this function. It is an energy-efficient system of asymmetrical reflectors that provides a uniform wash of light.

Lighting Standards

The Illuminating Engineering Society (Kaufman, 1959) suggests the following levels of maintained lighting intensity (taking light loss factors into consideration; foot-candles measure the light falling on a surface equivalent to the number of candles placed 1 foot from the lighted surface):

- Public service desks: 50 foot-candles average measured horizontally
- Staff areas: 50 foot-candles average measured horizontally at the desktop
- Small conference room: 30–40 foot-candles measured horizontally at the desktop with dimmers for audiovisual presentations
- Large multipurpose room: 40 foot-candles average with all lights on and separately controlled lighting from the front of the room (lighting dimmable to 2 foot-candles for note taking during audiovisual presentations)
- Reading areas: 30–40 foot-candles measured horizontally at the desktop

These figures do not always translate into visual acuity. Factors such as glare from bright lamps, presence of light-absorbing materials on the floor and walls, and contrast can dramatically affect people's perception of lighting levels.

For meeting rooms, light dimmers are especially useful to vary the intensity of light depending on the program content. The controls for these should be mounted near the stage or speaker area in the front of the room, and there should be separate light controls for:

- Stage or podium
- Audience
- Aisles

Theatrical lighting is expensive and requires elaborate ceiling racks and special wiring. The fixtures also produce considerable heat.

Fast Lighting or Slow Lighting

Lighting affects behavior. Bright, glary lighting is used in fast food stores to encourage people to leave the store quickly. Low-glare, softer light encourages people to stay and is appropriate in many areas of the library. Quiet study areas for long-term use need low-glare lighting, while the checkout desk lighting needs to be brighter to encourage quick staff response to waiting customers.

Chapter Summary

This chapter discusses the need to provide a powerful entrance experience by showing the variety of spaces within the children's area and emphasizing both openness and quiet spaces. Designers are encouraged to use a variety of display fixtures to show the front covers of children's materials and to link displays to task lighting. Graphics for the children's library should combine Dewey numbers with subjects in signage connected with the book stacks.

Reference

Kaufman, J., ed. 1959. *Illuminating Engineering Society Lighting Handbook,* 3rd edition. New York: Illuminating Engineering Society.

7

Age-Related Design

This chapter is about how the ages of children affect the design of their functional spaces. Children ranging from toddlers to young adults use the library in special ways that should be reflected in the design of the space. For example, book bins (Figure 7-1) are much easier for young children to browse through than book stacks, and teenagers will not want to walk through a space designed for children to reach the young adult section of the library.

Designing for Young Children

A variety of conflicting objectives should be considered:

- Children need help finding books but also need to be encouraged to pick out their own materials.
- Children need room to roam and places for shelter.
- Children's staff, parents, and caregivers need to find materials easily.

The Learning Experience

Young children are usually brought to the library by parents and caregivers, and library staff are often there to help. For a number of children, this may be their first visit, and they might find the library a strange and unusual place. They should quickly realize that they can get help and have some fun too.

Parents, caregivers, and library staff will want to share their experience of the materials in this resource-rich environment. Children's library staff are highly trained and experienced in finding age-appropriate materials that children enjoy, but children should be able to find materials easily and quickly on their own. Therefore, materials need to be in age-appropriate sequences on easy-to-reach shelves with appropriate signage indicating subject and Dewey Decimal number.

Children also need to be encouraged to help themselves and to discover that library collections are for browsing and for finding favorite subjects and authors. Librarians can help children to use the signs that explain the various subject and age-related sections. Signs should include Dewey Decimal numbers with pictorial symbols to help children locate their favorite subjects. Librarians can help children learn how to use the Dewey Decimal System.

Figure 7-1
Children at picture book bins at the Hartford (CT) Public Library,
designed by Michael Cohen of FHCM of Boston, MA.

Different Activity Levels

Infants, toddlers, and preschoolers act in different ways. At one moment they may be racing around the room, and then quietly settle down with a book. It is important to have spaces to accommodate these behaviors.

Children need an open area so they can roam around (like the one shown in Figure 7-2). Separate quiet areas (like that shown in Figure 7-3) function as "stimulus shelters" where toddlers can find quiet and security. Such areas serve a protective function by providing shelter from overstimulation for children who need relief from the noise and activity of the open area.

Children's Collections

There are several collections of books in the preschool area. In addition to the general Fiction and Nonfiction categories, shelving units accommodate the physical characteristics that are specific to children's books.

Bin shelving, which can have whimsical designs (see Figure 7-4), holds picture books. Alphabetical labels are placed on each bin. Children's picture books and board books have very thin spines, with tiny, almost invisible lettering that is very hard to read. In addition, young children are often not very good readers. Publishers realize these limitations and use pictures on the front covers to attract young children and their parents. Some libraries recognize the attraction of the front covers and the difficulties of reading the spine, so they shelve these materials in bins designed to have

**Figure 7-2
Room to roam—Picture book area at the Hartford (CT) Public Library,
designed by Michael Cohen of FHCM of Boston, MA.**

the book covers facing the browser. Alphabetical dividers may be used to make finding and sorting easier. Bins do not hold as many books per square foot of floor space as standard or divider shelving, but they will increase circulation.

Toddler sections will have board books in colorful cubes. Easy-reading books will be housed in shelving low enough for children to reach but not too low for grandparents and less mobile adults. Oversized books can be housed in a sloping shelf display (see Figure 7-5). Chapter books with thicker spines and large spine printing may be housed in regular shelving. Multimedia displayers on mobile carts are used to create temporary displays of books and other materials.

Furnishing for Young Children

Furnishings should have no sharp corners. Seating should include a rocking chair, perhaps a motorcycle or horse rocker, and large and oversized chairs for parents to sit with their children to read

**Figure 7-3
Children's shelter area at the Derby Neck (CT) Public Library, designed by George Buchanan (photo by Mary Beth Mahler).**

Figure 7-4
Train-shaped picture book bins at the Wallingford (CT) Public Library,
designed by Bruce Tuthill.

stories together. Tables and chairs should vary in size (for specifications, see Chapter 9). Some libraries provide a cradle or crib for infants, but these may need to be sanitized. Low floor tables (about 10 inches high) with cushions may also be considered here.

Figure 7-5
Slanting book display bin shelving at an English library.

Small children love the feeling of "looking down on the world." They welcome the opportunity to be just a little bit higher than the world around them. A small-scale, low, carpeted platform for them to climb up on can provide this experience (see Figure 7-6). To minimize injury, a triple-padded carpeted area should be installed at the foot of the platform. The fabric on the edges of the platform should be in a contrasting color, and there should be a ramp for access by children with disabilities. The location of this platform needs to be carefully chosen to avoid proximity to heavy traffic areas and to ensure the safety of children.

In contrast, sunken pits are sometimes used to vary the floor height. These are more permanent than platforms and are less flexible for future

Figure 7-6
Story platform at the Southbury (CT) Library, designed by Peter Wells
of Tuthill and Wells Architects of Avon, CT.

change. Changes in floor height need to be clearly identified; otherwise, they may create tripping hazards.

Electronic workstations may be grouped together in mezzitas (see Figure 7-7). The height levels of these units can be adjusted.

Children's areas should also have a collection of parenting, professional, and reference materials located in a conversational area (see Figure 7-8). Parents, teachers, child care and homeschool providers, as well as children will use this area. In addition to the collection, it will have adult-sized tables and chairs. Parents may also use this area to wait for children attending programs.

The library may want to create a caregiver commons with coffee service and an opportunity for discussion with other caregivers on topics of shared interest. The commons can also offer copies of parenting magazines and a few adult paperbacks of general interest.

Restrooms for children need changing tables, should be designed as family restrooms, and should be large enough and equipped for family use. Appropriately sized water fountains should be located nearby.

Plants and fish tanks are a wonderful way of introducing young people to the natural world, especially in urban libraries. They can be combined with book displays to show children how books can be useful guides to this natural world. Dewey Decimal numbers can be used to label plants and fish to show young children that these numbers have a relationship to finding things.

Figure 7-7
Mezzita computers by Totalibra provide electronic workstations designed especially for small children at the Hartford (CT) Public Library.

Figure 7-8
Separate area for parents and professionals at the Hartford (CT) Public Library, designed by Michael Cohen of FHCM of Boston, MA.

Designing for Older Children

This section focuses on design considerations for library spaces planned for older children. Differentiating this area from the younger children's area complements the older child's growing sense of identity and maturity.

Need for Differentiation of Spaces

Older children often complain that the children's areas are designed just for little kids. Older children should not need to walk through the small children's area to reach their space, and smaller children should not wander through the older children's area to reach their space. Ideally there will be two separate entrances.

The older children's areas should be welcoming to new users who have never been to a library before. On the other hand, veteran users who have just migrated from the area for younger children should find this area different and useful for independent study because they know how libraries work.

Older children may want to use younger children's material if they are dealing with a subject unfamiliar to them, and they may want to use adult materials when they have exhausted the children's collection on a subject. This dilemma may be solved by inter-filing children's, young adult, and adult nonfiction collections into a single sequence and identifying children's and young adult materials with spine labels.

Browsing and Reading

Children's areas designed for older children will be more traditional than those for younger children and will accommodate more directed activity. The following elements need to be incorporated:

- Display racks for newly published emergent-reader books, juvenile Fiction and Nonfiction books, and CDs and DVDs
- Display shelving for magazines and paperbacks
- A variety of seating and table heights
- Electronic workstations isolated from quiet study areas (see Figure 7-9)
- Portable computer and laptop units with a wireless router

The book stacks will be much larger than those provided for young children. Several design techniques will help make the book stack area more attractive:

- Display the front covers of interesting books on the end panels or top shelf (see Figure 7-10).
- Direct task lighting at the books, not the aisles.
- Use line-of-sight subject signs to indicate where subjects are located; include their Dewey numbers.
- Install sliding pullout shelves to rest books on to make stand-up browsing convenient and comfortable.
- Make aisles as wide as possible. The standard handicapped accessible aisle width of 40 inches may be too narrow. Space ranges (rows of connected shelves)

Figure 7-9
Computer area for older children at the Salt Lake City (UT) Library, designed by Moshe Safdie (photo by Jeff Hoover of Tappe Associates in Boston, MA).

Figure 7-10
Using end panel display boxes enhances visual interest.

72 inches from the center of one range to the center of the next range; this will leave an aisle 52 inches wide if 10-inch shelving is installed.

- Use a resilient flooring material, such as cork or vinyl, instead of carpeting to help illuminate the lower shelves. Place light fixtures above the aisles and directed toward the books.

Pegs on which to hang coats and small units in which to store backpacks should be distributed throughout the room but be convenient to seating places. Pegs may not be needed in warmer climates.

Functional Areas for Older Children

STUDY AND HOMEWORK AREAS

The study area should be near the Reference section for ease of access by children doing their homework. The study area should have individual computer workstations (see Figure 7-11) and collaborative electronic workstations where two people can work together. (The design of electronic workstations is discussed in more detail in Chapter 9.)

Low individual carrels should be located in a quiet area. A photocopier with a copy counter should be nearby but sound isolated. Study areas for individuals should be in a separate zone from group study areas. The zones can be differentiated by book stacks or sound-absorbing partitions.

Figure 7-11
Individual computer stations at the Hartford (CT) Public Library, designed by Michael Cohen of FHCM of Boston, MA.

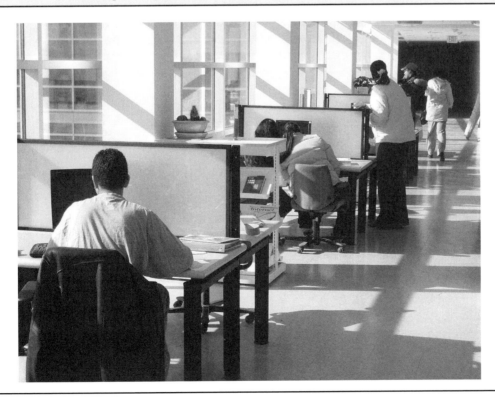

GROUP STUDY AREAS

Young people love to work together, especially to show off their computer skills. Note how crowded the group study area is in Figure 7-12. Ideally, groups of four children should be able to work together comfortably.

AFTER-SCHOOL ACTIVITIES

After-school activities include recreational programs and tutoring programs. These activities require an acoustically separated space. If space allows, tutorial rooms for individual consultation with children are desirable.

In some libraries, especially if they are within walking distance of a school, it may be necessary to plan for mobile seating and table groupings for 25 or more seats to accommodate a class.

Science in the Stacks Project at the Queens Borough Public Library

The Science in the Stacks project integrates hands-on experiences of basic science into the fabric of children's libraries. By bringing a flexible set of exhibits and activities to the "information toolkit" of a modern children's library, the Science in the Stacks concept expands and deepens science learning opportunities for children aged 3 to 12 years, especially those typically underserved by science experiences.

Science in the Stacks is a major element in the Children's Library Discovery Center (CLDC) at the Central Library of the Queens Borough Public Library system. The CLDC

Figure 7-12
Children working together at computers at the Keene (NH) Library, designed by Jeff Hoover of Tappe Associates, Boston, MA.

is an innovative concept in library youth services that recognizes that many children learn best through concrete experiences. It extends the evolving environment of a children's library by integrating direct, hands-on experiences in the sciences, arts, and humanities with reading and computer explorations to create a rich, multisensory learning environment.

The innovative elements that constitute the Science in the Stacks project include the following:

- Discovery Exhibits: Smaller versions of classic hands-on exhibits found in museums, Discovery Exhibits are roughly the size of a suitcase and can be relocated by library staff (but not customers). They are fully self-contained units that, unlike classic "discovery boxes" or other "kits," are closer in spirit to typical hands-on exhibits, only smaller, with a minimum of loose parts and no consumable supplies.
- Learning Cart: Mobile sets of activities for focused demonstrations or activities, these carts allow for more open-ended activities. Unlike the Discovery Exhibits, they will feature a higher-tech tool, such as a video microscope or a high-speed video recorder with a slow-motion playback option. Library staff may use these carts with library customers either on the library floor among the exhibits and books or in a closed Learning Lab supported by scripted activities drawn from science centers.

The San Francisco–based company Exploratorium for a fee will work with libraries to design an interactive learning center. They have produced a wide range of publications to assist in designing and constructing exhibits. They designed the exhibits incorporated into the Children's Library Discovery Center (see Figure 7-13).

Designing Young Adult Services

This section includes design tips that differentiate this part of the library from areas designed specifically for younger children so that young adults will be encouraged to come to the library.

What Teenagers Want

In focus groups, teenagers articulate their ideas about teen library service. The following excerpts are representative of what teenagers themselves had to say (the complete focus group reports are in Appendix A):

- There should be constant music in the teen library.
- We want a place for teens only, no younger kids.
- The library should be downtown and it should have:
  ○ Group study rooms
  ○ Places to talk
  ○ Homework corner
  ○ Laptop computers and Wi-Fi zone

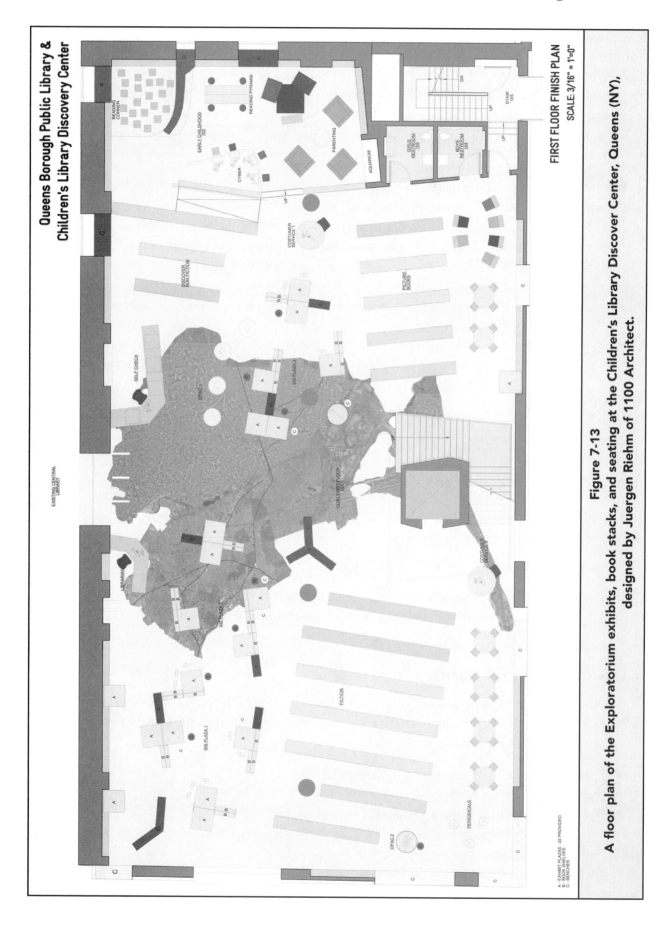

Figure 7-13

A floor plan of the Exploratorium exhibits, book stacks, and seating at the Children's Library Discover Center, Queens (NY), designed by Juergen Riehm of 1100 Architect.

- ○ Vending machines for snacks and drinks
- ○ Downloading of music and CD exchange
- ○ MySpace instant messaging
- ○ Teen volunteer tutors (other teens, not adults)
- ○ Friday night videos at the library
- ○ Contests and prizes, chess and checkers, free temporary tattoos
- ○ Teen night at the library with bands
- The library should be so nice that we want to be there for fun, not that you have to, just that you want to.
- The young adult library should be a reading room. Teens lose interest in the library after the fourth grade. We need a special place for middle-school kids. However, kids' books are easier to understand, so sometimes for basic subjects that we don't know a lot about it's better to start with the children's books. We need more Nonfiction in the teen area. Kids' books are just for fun.
- Put the kids' books near the adult books so adults and kids can read one another's books. Perhaps there could be separate shelves but not separate rooms. Why not put picture books in the adult section so little kids can browse with their parents? What about a reading room with glass doors and sound-absorbing materials so that people could use their laptops, TVs, and books all in the same room?
- Perhaps materials could all be integrated but the reading room separated by age. How about one large open space but separate teens and kids sections in the open space.
- How do we get people to like books? More storytimes for teens and adults. Headphones for music.
- The library needs to broadcast that it's there. Advertise libraries and books. Feature books that have been turned into movies. Change the view of what teenagers do. TEENAGERS READ.
- Make reading illegal, then all the teens will like it.
- Let people rate and comment on books they are reading right in the library's online catalog and Web site.

These comments confirm the basic ideas developed in this book for the design of teen space in libraries.

Involve Teenagers in the Design Process

First and foremost, involve teens in the design and selection of furniture and equipment. Architects and interior designers are essential to pull together the various design ideas suggested by teens, but the teens themselves will be articulate and inventive in their preferences, which should form the basis of the design.

Teenagers come to the library for several widely differing purposes, and they will alternate between different sets of activities. Conflicting uses require careful acoustical design to allow noisy and quiet activities to be acoustically separated from other areas, but close to adult materials.

For teenagers, libraries are a place to socialize. The library service needs of teenagers include space for social activities as well as space for age-appropriate materials and studying. Teens should feel that the library welcomes them and provides opportunities for them to socialize as well as study quietly. Design considerations include the following:

- Teenagers come to meet friends.
- An area designed for conversation, perhaps including a small coffee and snack service area, would be enjoyed by many teens.
- Teens often study in groups, so areas designed for four to six people would be welcome.

For teenagers, libraries are a place to listen to music. Multitasking is endemic with teenagers. They like to listen to music while working at their computers. Music is very important for teens, especially music they can share. Close proximity to the attractive display of new materials, especially music, would be welcome.

Libraries are a place to read. Teen materials such as graphic novels and anime are particularly attractive to teens, but they will also use adult materials.

Space in a library can be made appealing to teenagers by including the following functional zones and furnishings:

- A recreational use area with banquettes like a local diner
  - Constantly changing CDs, DVDs, books, and magazine displays
  - Art display area
  - Mobile bulletin boards
  - Comfortable lounge seating with low tables
  - Mobile viewing and listening stations
  - Food service area
- A study area
  - Oversized study tables with four chairs each
  - Individual electronic workstations (see Chapter 9 on furnishings and equipment for electronic workstation design)

An interesting teen library built in Phoenix, Arizona, and designed by Will Bruder, features a "teen café" (see Figure 7-14).

**Figure 7-14
Teen Café Read sign at the Phoenix (AZ) Public Library, designed by Will Bruder.**

Chapter Summary

This chapter focuses on the needs of children at different ages. Younger children need open space as well as shelters from activity. Parents and caregivers need space to be with their children as well as to visit with one another. Furnishings should accommodate children's smaller sizes and their increased need for safety. Older children require adequately sized electronic workstations and book stacks arranged by subject. Group study areas are an important feature for older children. For teenagers, the best sources of information about what they want are the teenagers themselves.

8

Designing Program, Activity, and Staff Areas

This chapter presents design considerations in planning functional areas for both children and staff (see also Chapter 10 on "quick fixes" if working with minimal resources). It discusses location and function to allow for both convenience and flexibility and also describes the features needed within each area.

Activities and Program Areas

This section reviews design considerations in planning for multipurpose program areas. Activities can range from quiet storyhours to active crafts.

Location

The multipurpose area may be located at the entrance of the children's library so that large numbers of children entering the program area will not disturb individuals studying in the children's room. It may also be located at the rear of the room to separate this activity. A rear location may require a sound-controlled passageway.

Acoustical Separation

The multipurpose area should be separated acoustically to keep noise from entering other areas. Use acoustical dividers to resize the area for smaller or larger audiences, as needed, and to divide the space for simultaneous programs. Complete acoustical separation may require a more expensive motorized divider.

Multimedia Facilities

Multimedia facilities are for viewing and listening to videos, music, and audiotapes individually and in small groups and for playing with board games, puzzles, toys, and computer games. They will include the following:

- Display tower with several screens for silent display of multimedia
- Storage and display for games, puzzles, toys, and multimedia kits
- Listening and viewing stations for audio and filmstrip kits

- Computers with printers on lock-and-roll storage carts
- Ceiling video projection equipment and ceiling-mounted screen

Storyhour Area

In addition to reading programs, other activities that take place in the storyhour area include puppet shows, creative dramatics, author talks, book groups, and video viewing. The following features can be included:

- A small, portable raised stage area with a ramp for handicapped access
- Stackable chairs
- Floor cushions or a stepped platform
- Cubbies for backpack storage (near the entrance)
- Performance area with modest stage-lighting capabilities
- Spotlight for storytellers
- Portable puppet stage

Video viewing will require curtains to control the level of sunlight in the room while maintaining dim ambient lighting for safety; children should never be in a completely dark room. The floor should be carpeted for both comfort and noise reduction.

Children may have to use larger adult facilities for extraordinarily large children's programs, so the children's area should be located near the adult program room.

Crafts Area

It is desirable to have a separate crafts area (see Figure 8-1). Some activities can be messy. Supplies need to be carefully monitored and inaccessible when not being used.

The activity area for crafts may have the following:

- Easily cleaned flooring, with a floor drain, if possible
- Sink, counter, and lockable storage for materials
- Space for children to move around
- Lighting for close construction work
- Mobile trash containers for easy cleanup
- Adjustable-height folding tables
- Storage for chairs and tables

Some craft areas may even incorporate a kitchen unit containing a refrigerator, stove, sink, serving counter, garbage can, and lockable storage (see Figure 8-2). Recyclable materials should be separated from other garbage.

Space Dividers

In smaller libraries, the multipurpose area may have to be created for each program by moving book stacks, chairs, and tables. For this reason, keep the stacks low to lessen their weight to a movable capacity, perhaps no taller than 42 inches. Wider aisles may also be necessary to allow book stacks to be moved into book stack aisles to achieve the open space needed for programs.

Figure 8-1
Crafts area at the Wallingford (CT) Public Library, designed by Bruce Tuthill.

Figure 8-2
Example of how a kitchen unit was incorporated into the craft area at the Salt Lake City (UT) Public Library (photo by Jeff Hoover of Tappe Associates).

In larger libraries, the multipurpose areas may be located in separate rooms. In the largest public libraries, the craft area may be separated from the storyhour facility. The following design considerations are applicable to libraries of all sizes:

- Book stacks make excellent sound-absorbing dividers.
- Partition walls on wheels can be relocated at will to create separate areas for informal small-scale activities with only a few children participating.
- Sliding partitions on tracks provide acoustical barriers that allow for two programs to occur at the same time.

Library Staff Service and Work Areas

This section reviews design criteria for service desks, staff work areas, and library storage areas. Efficient use of space for staff improves the overall functionality of the children's area.

Service Desk

LOCATION

The location of the service desk (see Figure 8-3) may vary depending on the size of the children's area, the functions that take place at the desk, and, most important, the location of any building exit that may be in the vicinity. In some libraries, especially those in which the children's area is close to the exit from the library building, for

Figure 8-3
Children's service desk at the Hartford (CT) Public Library.

safety and security reasons, the children's service desk will be located close to the exit and to the toddlers' area.

The children's service desk should be visible upon entering the area and should provide good supervision of the entire area to prevent children from leaving the building and running into the street. In larger libraries, the service desk may be located closer to the center of the room, so that staff can more easily move to all parts of the area, but it should still be visible from the entrance. This may also be the case when the children's area is on a nonentrance floor or far from the entrance.

FUNCTIONS

The service desk usually functions as a place where staff can both check materials in and out and assist children. If materials are checked in and out here, the desk may need to have dual-height areas; staff can perform checkout activities behind the higher transaction area, and children, parents, and caregivers can rest their materials on the top of the counter (see Figure 8-4). The checkout function will also require space for book trucks to keep checked-in materials ready for shelving.

Computer space on the desk also will be needed. Staff will use the computers to find materials and answer questions. A printer and telephones will also be needed. A large display calendar or flat-screen monitor may list children's events.

Underneath the service counter, all sections should be on mobile carts independent of the desk structure so that they can be reconfigured easily. These carts are used to hold materials for a variety of staff needs.

**Figure 8-4
Inside a children's service desk at the Hartford (CT) Public Library.**

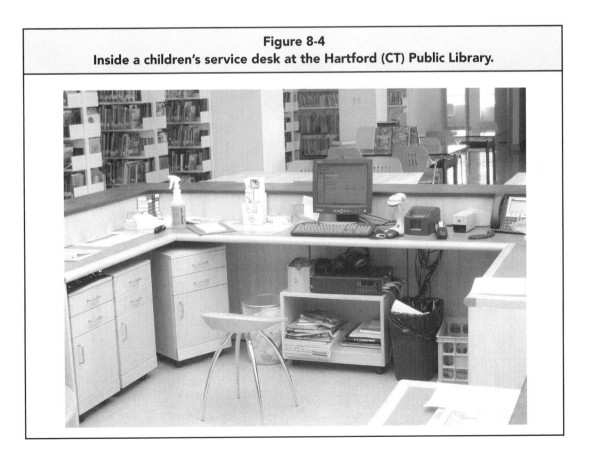

Service desk height is an issue, especially for smaller children. A solution may be to provide a small step stool, but this may be a safety hazard and will not be useful for children with disabilities. A better solution is to design the service desk with varying heights to accommodate different-sized children. Some newer desks can be designed with adjustable-height devices that raise or lower the desk height at the touch of a button. Book displays may be built into the front of the service desk (see Figure 8-5).

Work Area

It is essential that all staff members have a dedicated space where they can work. The staff work area is often located close to the service desk to allow observation of active areas, especially in small libraries where staff have to perform a variety of functions. In small libraries the work area will include partitioned space for the children's librarian.

In larger libraries, the staff work area may be located away from the service desk in order to monitor another part of the children's area. Larger libraries may also have a separate office for the children's librarian.

The staff work area will have electronic workstations with Internet access, a printer, and an arts and crafts space with sink, design table, and counter for laminating equipment. Storage will hold a variety of materials and supplies. Working materials will be kept in storage cabinets or on adjustable bookshelves or counters.

The arrangement of work spaces, the location of equipment, acoustical dampening, lighting, and color scheme should promote productivity and attention to detail over long periods of time. The staff area may have operable windows and curtains, to adjust for privacy. Natural lighting from windows should be augmented by task lighting. These should have flexible switching patterns.

Figure 8-5
Circulation desk at the King of Prussia (PA) Library, designed by Diseroad and Wolf Architects, Hatfield, PA.

Space for individual expressions, such as a shelf for potted plants and wall space for posters and holiday decorations, promote an atmosphere of comfort. Cork bulletin boards or a tackable surface should be placed at workstations so that staff can easily refer to schedules, procedural memos, and other temporary notes. All work areas need coat racks and lockers for employees' personal possessions.

Climate control is essential for staff who spend long hours at workstations. Staff should be able to control their own climate.

Natural lighting from windows is important for the morale of the staff. Avoid under-shelf lighting. Glare can be a major problem, and overly dim lighting can cause staff to strain to read a computer screen or paper documents on the desk. Lighting that is adequate during the day may be completely inadequate in the evening. Because proper lighting is relative, adjustability in task lighting at the workstation is important. Workers are more productive when they can adjust the intensity, location, and the angle of light in their work area.

Chairs, work surfaces, and other furnishings must be ergonomically designed and provide good support, especially to the sacrolumbar area of the workers' backs.

The staff area might have the appearance of a small house within the library, with operable double-hung windows and curtains to adjust for the privacy of workers within the work area.

Storage

Storage areas should be in close proximity to the service desk. Storage areas will hold such items as flannel boards, coats and personal belongings of the staff, and office supplies. Children's facilities need additional storage spaces for items particular to children's services:

- Seasonal materials in demand at particular times of the year
- Audiovisual equipment
- Craft and storyhour materials
- Folding chairs and tables
- Puppet stage and hand puppets
- Posters, prints, and mobiles

Figure 8-6 illustrates how storage spaces can be separate from actual work spaces yet be conveniently close by.

Chapter Summary

This chapter focuses on the design considerations when planning library space for multipurpose and staff areas. Children's spaces for storyhours, craft activities, puppet shows, creative dramatics, parenting programs, discussions, author talks, book groups, and video viewing should reflect the need for both story and craft functions. The chapter presents techniques for dividing large spaces when separate rooms are not available.

Figure 8-6
Staff work room that includes storage space at the Hartford (CT) Public Library,
designed by Michael Cohen of FHCM architects, Boston, MA.

This chapter also emphasizes the need for dedicated staff work spaces within the children's area, including ample storage for materials used in the variety of children's programs and activities. Service desks should provide for book displays and differentiate between users and staff by including dual-height counters. Flexibility results from designing a shell desk with movable inserts.

9

Furnishings and Equipment

This chapter discusses the appropriate sizes and types of children's furnishing required to create an environment for children that is best suited and most comfortable for them. We also discuss the mobility and durability of library equipment as well as active and quiet zone considerations. Contact information for suppliers of the different types of furniture and equipment discussed is provided in Appendix E.

Entrance

Children should experience the magic of libraries from the moment they arrive (see Figure 9-1). Effective use of furnishings at the entrance can set the stage for the experience to come. Figures 9-2 and 9-3 illustrate how the entrance design of the Martin Library, in York, Pennsylvania, creates the entrance experience.

Active Zones

Active zones are often located near the entrance. They should be an open play space environment for children to make-believe in. Oversized chairs should be available so that parents and children can sit together and look at books. A section of the seating in this zone should accommodate parents and caregivers visiting with one another, so there should be low tables close by for purses, personal belongings, and library materials.

There may be stand-alone computers for quick lookups and collaborative electronic workstations large enough for a librarian and a child to sit side by side. This active area should have a spotlighted display for a wide variety of media so that children can browse through attractively displayed materials.

Low floor tables, 12 inches high, with floor cushions are useful for small kids. Foam pieces in various shapes, such as cubes, mushrooms, or rockers, are also handy for small kids.

Small children like variations in height. A low platform can offer a memorable experience for a small child to get up a little higher and look down on some other activity. However, these height variations require handicapped accessibility with ramps, and care should be taken to make entering these height variations a safe experience, with thickly padded carpet and contrasting floor coloring to signal the height variation.

Figure 9-1
Service desk at the Greenwich (CT) Public Library, designed by Cesar Pelli, architect.

Figure 9-2
House and trees greet children coming to the Martin Library in York, PA, designed by Robert Kinsley, architect, of York, PA.

Figure 9-3
Huge books are part of the entrance experience at the Martin Library, York, PA.

Furnishings and equipment should be mobile. They can be mounted on wheels or gliders so that staff can change the layout of the area for a variety of different activities during the day.

Quiet Zones

Subdued lighting and furnishings in calming colors should indicate to children that another part of the library is for long-term quiet study. Individual, widely spaced study carrels provide a quiet space and relief from the active noisy zone. When possible, windows in this part of the library should look out onto a quiet garden scene.

Workstations and Study Areas

Oversized collaborative electronic workstations are useful near the service desk for assisting children unfamiliar with searching and for assistance with complex searches.

**Figure 9-4
Data tower by Totalibra.**

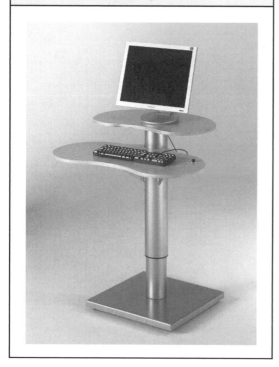

Stand-up computer stations are useful for staff to quickly locate materials or to answer brief reference questions (see Figure 9-4). These stations should be available at the entrance and throughout the book stacks. Biomorph, Highsmith, and other manufacturers offer "hi-lo" workstations, which can be adjusted to either a sitting or a standing configuration. Electronic workstations designed to meet library workers' specific needs are discussed in more detail later in this chapter.

Make individual study carrels visible down the stack aisles so that a child selecting a book has ready access to a place to read it. If carrels are located far from supervision, they should be single carrels spaced far apart to discourage talking.

Table Seating

Small 3- by 5-foot tables discourage use by more than two people (see Figure 9-5). Larger 4- by 6-foot tables are more likely to be used by four people.

**Figure 9-5
Electronic workstation at the Hartford (CT) Public Library,
designed by Michael Cohen of FHCM Architects, Boston, MA.**

Alcove arrangements with low shelves on three sides of a reading table are highly desired for privacy and to separate user groups.

Study Rooms

Study rooms are essential for collaborative study and teaching activities. They should be equipped with computer network connections. White boards are useful for communication among small groups.

Seating Design Considerations

Children need a wide range of choices in seating because they come in different sizes and forms and use libraries in different ways. A sedentary 60-pound child coming to the library for several days of research has different needs than a restless 100-pound teenager coming to listen to the latest CD.

Chairs are the most important pieces of equipment in the library. They should be the first priority in equipment budgets, and there should be no compromise for comfort and durability. Many library patrons will sit for hours of intensive study, and their comfort will determine their level of satisfaction with the library study experience. If libraries want to distinguish themselves from bookstores, chair comfort can be an important factor in that distinction.

**Figure 9-6
Iconic stool designed by
Alvar Aalto of Finland.**

Scale

One of the most important factors in selecting children's furniture is scale. Children's tables and chairs typically come in two sizes. According to Graham and Demmers (2005: 25):

> Juvenile tables are typically 27" high and pre-school tables are typically 21–24" high. A few manufacturers have more options, with heights of 16", 18", 20", or 25". The corresponding seat heights on chairs are typically 16" high for juveniles and 13–14" high for children. Whichever is selected, the table and the chair must be in the same scale and most critically allow a dimension of 9–10" between seat height and table height. If a chair designed for an adult is to be scaled down for children and juveniles, it is not enough to merely lower the seat. The seat saddle should also be scaled down, as should the back height to provide comfortable seating for smaller bodies. This is also true of stools used as seating. Frequently children's chairs are available without a back, a feature that makes the chair more stable and less prone to tip over. Children's chairs should be designed not to rock or tip over.

**Figure 9-7
Kin-der-Link stools.**

Figures 9-6 and 9-7 illustrate two options for children's chairs. Regardless of size, type, or location, children's furnishings should be chosen for their ability to stand considerable use and to be easily repaired.

Comfort

Chair comfort is not simply a function of hard or soft surfaces. In fact, hard surfaces shaped carefully to human bone structure may be more comfortable than rectangular slabs of foam. Chairs that afford patrons the opportunity to both move within the chair and move the chair itself will be preferred over handsomely sculptured stiff shapes such as the Barcelona chair.

People spend a great deal of time in library chairs. Therefore, chairs should be extremely comfortable and conform to the human body. Ergonomically designed chairs not only conform to the curve of the back but also provide side-to-side support for the lower back. It is important to get in and out of a chair with ease. Pregnant women and older people may experience difficulty getting out of low lounge chairs. People vary in size, so a variety of chair designs should be available. Woven fabric tends to be more breathable than vinyl and more comfortable to sit in.

Adjustability

Seat height is adjustable, usually with a gas cylinder lever on the side of the chair. The cylinder should be easy to replace when it malfunctions. Lower back lumbar support should be firm and adjustable up and down. The seat back should move with the body and be adjustable back and forth for different tasks. An electronic workstation should be equipped with a chair that supports the back in an upright position, while a lounge chair in the magazine reading area should recline and support the back as the reader's body moves. Chairs should accommodate movement of the body. The chair should flex and support the body as it moves within the chair.

Durability and Cost

Library chairs tend to sustain many years of regular use, up to 12 hours a day, up to 7 days a week. It is difficult to find an inexpensive chair that will hold up and still be handsome over this span of time. Hundreds of people will use the chairs each day; therefore, it is important to select fabrics, materials, and structures that will last a long time. Carefully examine wood frames for their construction before making a decision as to their durability. The Eustis chairs, with their epoxy-injected gluing system, are a good example of a durable wooden chair.

Lounge Chairs

The Stressless reclining chair and footstool, constructed of tubular steel and leather upholstery with a curved foam back, is an extremely comfortable chair that can be easily adjusted to fit any size person. It is also relatively easy to get in and out of.

Task Chairs

Mobile task chairs for electronic workstations are available in a wide variety of price ranges. The Charles Perry Uno chair is adjustable in height, flexes, and moves with the user (see Figure 9-8).

The Herman Miller Aeron chair is an ergonomic design classic and is the standard chair used in the Science, Industry and Business Branch of the New York Public Library. It has a ventilated seat and back to prevent heat buildup. The Steelcase Criterion chair has a back that moves in and out for lumbar support for working at a computer. The Leap chair by Steelcase has a height-adjustable lumbar support for the lower back.

Carpet-Compatible Design

Purchase chairs that are on casters or have a runner on the bottom so that they can glide easily on carpet. Heavy wooden four-legged chairs are harder to move and difficult to pull back from a table when standing up. They may also damage the carpet in a short time. They often tip over when they are tilted back. Two-position wooden chairs with increased stability and two-position bases are available.

Figure 9-8
Uno chair, designed by Charles Perry and manufactured by Turnstone (photo by Mary Beth Mahler of Lushington Associates).

Maintenance

Select height-adjustable chairs that have easily replaceable gas cylinders. Some furniture comes with upholstery that can be replaced by simply unscrewing the seat or back. Buttons or sling backs or Velcro on some lounge seating permits even faster replacement. Darnell-Rose casters on chairs facilitate easy movement.

Electronic Workstations for Staff

This section is based on work done by Dr. James Kusack at the Southern Connecticut State University School of Library Science in New Haven in 1989. It focuses on staff workstations. Workstations for library users are discussed earlier in this chapter.

Adjustability

All aspects of the workstation should be adjustable and adequate for staff with special problems, such as back problems, and those who wear eyeglasses. They should also be adjustable for people of different heights. This flexibility is critical because staff differ in size, bodily configuration, and work preferences.

Seating

The staff member should be able to adjust the height of the seat and the backrest. Furthermore, the backrest and seat pan should be laterally adjustable so that the user can move the backrest fore and aft and change the seat deflection from flat to a somewhat backward angle. All adjustment levers must be readily accessible and easy to use—staff should not have to turn chairs upside down to make adjustments. Hydraulic mechanisms are necessary where two or more people use the same workstation. Armrests should be adjustable and removable. The chair itself should move and swivel to allow the worker to perform a wide range of activities. Chairs should be designed for simple maintenance, including replacement of upholstery and mechanical controls.

Desks and Work Surfaces

Ideally library workers should have desks and work surfaces that can be adjusted from 22 to 45 inches from the floor. Normal desk height is 26 to 30 inches. The flexibility to raise the work surface to counter height permits workers with a back injury to use a keyboard or library materials while standing. Kneehole space should be available so that chairs can be out of the way when not needed.

At minimum, the work area must include an adjustable keyboard pan, which enables sitting workers to maintain their upper and lower arms at a 90-degree angle (upper arm vertical, forearm horizontal) and their wrists at 10 to 20 degrees from horizontal. A tilting keyboard pan would also help improve the wrist angle. Lack of adjustability may be a major cause of repetitive motion syndrome in those working at keyboards.

The ideal work area is 60 inches wide and at least 30 inches deep to permit opening books or using documents or other media. Leg clearance should be at least 24 inches wide and 16 inches deep. Space for book trucks at each workstation is imperative.

Computer Equipment

The librarian's role in the Information Age demands increased reliance on computers and related technology. Librarians create, maintain, and search local and remote databases; they use computers to write reports, letters, and other documents; and they use spreadsheets and other productivity software to plan budgets and manage the organization.

Local area networks and connectivity are important aspects of a library's ability to use this technology. Design features must reflect the need to power and connect equipment in each workstation as well as among the different departments. J-channels, ramps, grommeted openings for bundled cables, and power poles will be important design features.

The workstation will need room for a variety of hardware, including some bulky equipment like printers and paper supplies, and storage devices such as CDs and DVDs. Shelving for manuals and supporting documents is also important.

Screens

Placement of the monitor is a primary concern. The screen should be approximately 18 inches from the eyes and as low as possible. The screen should never be above normal eye level. The users should be able to raise, lower, tilt, and swivel the screen to suit their individual requirements.

Visual fatigue can be minimized by correct lighting. Artificial or natural light that is too bright can cause glare, so do not place monitors next to windows. When this is necessary, place the screen at a right angle to the plane of the window. Polarized glare screens may be helpful, and blinds also control reflected glare.

Cost

Purchasing workstations of this quality will benefit staff for years to come. Libraries that specify expensive marble checkout desks should not be reluctant to also spend money on user comfort. Prevention of repeated motion syndrome injuries to staff resulting from poor ergonomic design may more than compensate for the cost of an ergonomic chair and workstation. All equipment does not need to be in place on the day the new library opens. It can be phased in and purchased over a period of years.

Costs for well-designed workstations are also decreasing. The Charles Perry Uno chair and the Biomorph workstations do not cost much more than a good-quality study carrel and wooden chair.

Floors

Carpeting is the preferred library flooring material for its acoustical absorbency. It should be low pile (less than ¼ inch high), looped through the backing for durability under heavy book trucks, and have a minimum face weight of 25 ounces per square yard.

- Install different color and pattern carpeting in heavy use areas and plan to replace these areas more often than light use areas.
- Carpet tile may be useful for flat wiring access in small areas.
- Mixed tweed colors will look better than solid colors when dirty.
- Change colors to signal changes in floor height or zoning for activity differences.

Entrance mats should allow dirt to drop below the walking surface and should be easily removable for frequent cleaning.

Cork floors are durable and sound absorbent and have a high reflectance to increase light on the bottom shelves of book stacks.

Colorful fish or other decorations in carpets may have an interest for children who are closer to the floor than adults but may also look worn and dated in a short time.

Design Result

The children's area design should be an intriguing combination of creativity, function, and flexibility.

- Children should be engaged by areas that stimulate their imagination while suggesting a variety of behaviors.
- Alternating active and quiet environments offers children a choice.
- The area should be easy to change for short-term display and long-term changes in function as children change.
- Parents and other caregivers should have an opportunity to sit with children and to enjoy meeting with one another.

- There should be an opportunity for individual consultation with children.
- Children should be able to work together.
- Program space should have flexibility.

Chapter Summary

This chapter shows how furnishings for the active zone for younger children, parents, and caregivers should be mobile and light, while quiet zone furnishings for older children require ergonomic design for long-term comfort. Electronic workstation designs for children and staff require adjustability. Library chairs should be mobile and flexible and provide lumbar support for the lower back. Carpet and cork floors are compared. The chapter ends with a summary of design results that demonstrate the effect of good furniture selection.

Reference

Graham, Carole, and Linda Demmers. 2005. "Furniture for Libraries." Libris Design Project, funded by The Institute of Museum and Library Services, California. Available: www .librisdesign.org/docs/FurnitureLibraries.pdf.

10

Quick Fixes and Common Mistakes

This chapter presents suggestions for quick improvements with a minimum of resources to help existing libraries enhance their design and the overall library experience (see also the case study in Appendix B). This chapter also outlines some of the common mistakes when it comes to the design of a children's library.

Displays

Display the front covers of children's books. Publishers spend thousands of dollars hiring wonderful artists to design the front covers of children's books, and the American Library Association awards a prize to the best children's illustrator each year. Yet many libraries hide these front covers in spine-out shelves rather than finding opportunities to display them.

Book bins provide these display opportunities for thin picture books, which are often selected by children who do not yet know how to read and therefore cannot understand the tiny letters on the thin spines. Placing these displays at the entrance of the children's area is a good way to attract children to enter.

Librarians should change the displays at the beginning of each day. Nothing is more discouraging for children who come to the library often than to see the same old books.

Weeding

Beautiful gardens are weeded, and so are book collections. Children's libraries should not be crammed with materials that are not often used. Based on circulation statistics, identify and discard materials that have not been borrowed while retaining classics. Do not store little-used materials that can be accessed online.

Lighting

Spotlighting new materials makes them more attractive. This can sometimes be accomplished merely by selecting different light bulbs that can be put into existing fixtures. Full-spectrum fluorescent lamps are available that are not only more attractive but are actually more healthful than older, cool white lamps.

Swivelier makes fixtures that screw into existing high-hat recessed lights and have hanging rods that allow the light to be directed toward the books. Very narrow spotlights can highlight a particular book or seating location.

Collaboration

Local community theaters and museums offer libraries a wonderful array of collaborative opportunities that can help stimulate interest in both institutions and liven up the appearance and activities in the library. Suggestions on how different community groups can work together include the following:

- Share lists of books on theater productions.
- Invite the actors to give book readings.
- Offer the museum staff library materials and lists to go with their exhibits.
- Invite museum staff to give talks and readings at the library.

Common Mistakes and Simple Solutions

Most design flaws can be resolved quickly and with minimum expense. Some simple solutions to mistakes commonly found in libraries follow:

- Buried covers—There is insufficient display of front covers of children's books. No picture book bins are provided for browsing. Solution: Display front covers on bookshelves.
- Too many books—The library retains books that nobody wants to read, so there is not enough space for children. Solution: Get rid of the books nobody wants.
- Too many sections—The library has too many categories of books, making it hard for a child to find a particular item. Solution: Reduce the number of separately sequenced categories so that children can find books more easily, and use signs.
- Poor sequencing—Categories are not layed out logically, so subjects and authors are hard to find. Solution: Arrange materials in sequence with subject aisle signage, and avoid circular spinners.
- Narrow aisles—Stacks are spaced 5 feet apart instead of 6 feet, so parents and children feel crowded in the stacks. Solution: Widen the aisles.
- Poor lighting—Lighting is either too bright and glary or too dull. Solution: Change lamps and fixtures to modulate light according to need.
- No quiet area—There is no place that a child can go to read quietly. Solution: Rearrange book stacks and seating to create a quiet area, such as an alcove.
- Not enough change—The same books are on display every day, so children think the library is old and static. Solution: Change display books daily.
- Too "cute"—Displays of too many objects makes the library seem like a rummage room. Solution: Keep use of items other than library materials to a minimum.
- Insufficient staff storage—Staff areas are full of stuff, and there is insufficient storage space in the staff area. Solution: Discard nonessential items.

- Crowded electronic workstations—When electronic workstations are all lined up, the area feels like a classroom. Solution: Distribute electronic workststions throughout the library.

Chapter Summary

A children's library can be enhanced by implementing some basic lighting and display techniques to make the books more attractive and by installing comfortable chairs, tables, and ergonomically designed electronic workstations. Mistakes in designing children's libraries include ignoring front cover display opportunities, not changing displays often enough, and allowing spaces to become cluttered.

APPENDIX A

Focus Groups

This appendix presents comments by members of focus groups from a small suburban community and a larger town to demonstrate how children talk about libraries.

Seventh- and Eighth-Grade Focus Group

- The library should have anime clubs, gaming, and RuneScape programs.
- There should be constant music in the teen library.
- The library building is cold, not like Borders.
- We go to the Conservation Center swimming place or the mall to hang out.
- The library should be downtown near Main Street.
- We want a place for teens only, no younger kids.

The students identified numerous types of activities that they would like their libraries to offer:

- Crafts, duct tape parties, neon parties
- MySpace instant messaging
- Teen volunteer tutors (other teens, not adults)
- Free color printing
- Friday night movies at the library
- Teen book discussions
- Contests and prizes, chess and checkers, free temporary tattoos
- Harry Potter party
- Teen night at the library with bands
- CD exchange program

The students also identified the following physical features as desirable:

- Group study rooms
- Places to talk
- A homework corner
- Laptop computers and Wi-Fi zones
- Capability to download music
- Vending machines for snacks and drinks
- Bright colors

- Reading garden
- Different-sized tables for groups of two, four, and six people
- An open look
- Lounge chairs or bean bags or video rockers
- No fluorescent lights, and floor and table lamps that can be controlled
- Softer lights, not bright spotlights
- Special book lighting for the stacks
- Magazine section
- Loud room
- Movie room
- More graphic novels

Teenage Focus Group

- It's hard to find a book at this library. There's no place to sit. The young adult materials are too close to the kids' library. We need more tables, more room to hang out. The library should be so nice that we want to be there for fun, not that you have to, just that you want to.
- The young adult library should be a reading room. It should be enclosed in glass. There should be more space so people can get through, so that they can feel free to look at a book that they want.
- The children's room lacks the stuff you need. The junior library is so separate from the main library that it is not an easy transition for teens. Teens lose interest in the library after the fourth grade. We need a special place for middle-school kids. However, kids' books are easier to understand, so sometimes for basic subjects that we don't know a lot about it's better to start with the children's books. There are more children's Nonfiction books than teen Nonfiction. We need more Nonfiction in the teen area. Kids' books are just for fun. There should be few kids' books in the adult section as well as some audiovisual kids' stuff.
- Put the kids' books near the adult books so adults and kids can read one another's books. Now standing in the adult section you can't see kids. It should be easier to see the kids. Perhaps there could be separate shelves but not separate rooms. Why not put picture books in the adult section so little kids can browse with their parents? What about a reading room with glass doors and sound-absorbing materials so that people could use their laptops, TVs, and books all in the same room?
- What about alternating kids, adults, and teens? Perhaps materials could all be integrated, but the reading room separated by age. Right in the reading room there could be the multiple copies of books.
- How about one large open space but separate teen and kids sections in the open space, so all the people could be in the same room—a large public space open to all? Maybe that would be too mixed and confused.
- We need big chairs to sit in and read, parents and kids together.
- We like Borders because of the atmosphere. It's more relaxed, cleaner, with signs, open and airy, well lit, everything has its place. At Borders there is a big

selection, they have enough new books. At the library they have the same old books all the time.

- The library should have a recording studio for both video and sound.
- We like our middle school. It has lots of natural light and low shelves. The library should be quiet with headphones. The library should be an interactive space but not just for play and games. We should be able to talk with one another about books.
- There is a difference between books and manga graphic novels, which should be separated. The library is for materials, not like the teen center, which is just for play. The library is for learning. We should have a teen cultural center for different kinds of music, dance, drama, art. Learn something new every week about a different country. NOT a teen center.
- How do we get people to like books? More storytimes for teens and adults. Headphones for music. TV is bad. Send a new mother home from the hospital with a book to read to her new baby. The library should be more proactive and welcoming. Expand readers' knowledge of the world. People don't like books because they want instant gratification. The library should have book clubs to discuss books we are reading. The library needs to broadcast that it's there.
- I loved my field trip to the library when I was in school.
- We should have reading time for kids.
- Advertise libraries and books. Feature books that have been turned into movies.
- Change the view of what teenagers do. TEENAGERS READ!
- What is the homeless policy of the library?
- Teens are turned off by school reading, which is so dull.
- Why not read *Push*, the teenage online magazine.
- Make reading illegal—then all the teens will like it.
- Match everyone with a book they will enjoy.
- Let people rate and comment on books they are reading right in the library's online catalog and Web site.

Case Study of a Children's Room Analysis, Program, and Redesign

I founded Lushington Associates in 1970. It is a consulting firm specializing in improving library facilities. We have completed over 300 projects in 10 states. This appendix presents an actual case study of a project to redesign an existing library with extensive staff input but minimal resources. The goal was to work within existing spaces and not move walls.

Timeline

1. March 22: Lushington Associates will meet with the children's room staff to evaluate the present room arrangement and to discuss objectives for improvement.
2. Week of March 26: Preliminary sketches and alternative layouts will be drawn for the room.
3. March 28: Bids will open for the painting and carpeting of the area.
4. Week of April 2: Staff will finalize the layout.
5. Week of April 9: Furniture and equipment will be selected and added to the layout.
6. By April 10: A contract will be signed and work will proceed, with the children's area remaining open if possible.

Notes Recorded by Library Consultant During the Kickoff Meeting

- Staff will select materials for moving into storage to reduce collection size to be housed.
- Clear staff sight lines to presently concealed room areas is of some concern.
- She is open to the use of picture book bins.
- Small children and picture books to be located near staff service desk at entrance and near activity program room.
- Older children to be in distant quieter area.

- Minimum funds may be available for some new furniture and equipment after carpet and painting bids are opened, but most of the existing furniture will be reused and new added gradually as funds become available.
- Potential for mobile flexible staff workstation away from service desk, perhaps data tower design.
- More easily height-adjustable craft tables.
- Lighting is very poor with scattered fluorescent ceiling fixtures, some with missing lenses. No money available for new lighting at present.

Notes Recorded During Children's Staff Meeting

The staff identified the following aspects of the children's library that they like:

- The separate story and craft area has storage, sink, and bathroom.
- The small play area with an outside view looking into the courtyard is nice but too small, and children may get lost running into the courtyard when the door is open.
- There are separate well-defined areas with different vertical levels—noise and activity are contained within each area.
- The quiet study room is isolated from most noisy active areas, and it is large enough for groups.
- The service desk is close to the computers.
- The play area and picture books are together and close to the family bathroom.

The staff identified the following aspects that they don't like about the present area layout:

- The service desk is placed so that at times people enter the space behind the staff. The two entrances—staircase and ramp—make it hard to face two directions at once so that we can adequately greet users.
- Picture books are too far from the service desk.
- Computers should be separated from the homework study area so that kids doing homework do not hear the computer noise.
- Occasionally there is an unpleasant gasoline smell from outside.
- We hate the central albatross of an air-handling unit that dominates the entrance to the room.
- We need a pegboard wall for puppets and bags.
- There should be backing to the paperback shelves so that books don't fall off shelves.
- Lighting is often glary in some areas and sometimes insufficient in other areas.
- The service desk is too large, and it is not ergonomically designed.
- Not enough self-service signage.
- What should we do with the animal head displayer on the far wall?

The following objectives were set:

- Provide more space for quiet study and computers.
- Rearrange service desk in better relation to entrance.

- Have picture book and larger play area for younger children closer to staff and family bathroom.
- Clear passages and continue defining various activities.
- Create wider aisles, improve lighting for books and people, and open entry walls.

Notes from the Second Staff Meeting

- Meeting began outside.
- Toured the sidewalk, asking, What do you see and how do you see it? Then entered the library and walked toward the children's library.
- Visual exercises continued concerning viewpoints of signage, entrance, plus user's experience of the exterior, as in welcoming versus forbidding.
- Visual interior sights and comments:
  1. A very negative warning sign: "Your actions are being watched and recorded."
  2. Children's area signage too late in the pathway, too small, and too high.
  3. Suggest larger children's sign over the staff door to the basement with arrow and rainbow identifier.
  4. Noted: If the stairs into the children's staff area are removed or, worse, boarded over, the immediate view into the room will be lost.
  5. Consider book-lined passageways, walkway areas/ramps with front cover display of books in Lucite Beemak containers.
  6. Consider using the activity room for young children for better use of underutilized space.
  7. Perhaps kids visible from the street.
  8. Upper space (today's Nonfiction-computer area) for older children and book stacks/computer area.
  9. Virginia Hatch Room (with windows) felt to be a very special place; open it for reading area, casual seating, study carrels, a blend of seating choices; no tall stacks.
  10. Methodology of choosing a carpet by sprinkling carpet samples with the contents of vacuum cleaner bags.
  11. Discussed concepts of early planning formula and zone approach: What is the best matchup per zone (as in small children and book bins and mobile toy storage in same area)?
  12. Considered small/large changes: take small book carts rough-sorted to the area where they belong; later shelved if patrons haven't quickly scooped them up again.
  13. No longer a need for holding shelves and extra handling of books—save shelves, time, and labor—small change, big payout.

Children's Area Analysis

The children's facilities at this library have an interesting history. When the library purchased the bank next door to expand its children's programs, the library initiated an extensive daycare learning center program that was unique as a public library model. For this reason, the program facilities were extensive and heavily used. As time went by, the budget for these programs was somewhat reduced.

The library still has an extensive program of children's activities. With growing collections and the need for more electronic workstations and improved staff work facilities, it may be useful to look carefully at facilities' space allocations and to utilize part of the program area for day-to-day library activities as well as programs.

During the analysis phase, it is helpful to work with staff to prepare detailed Functional Area Sheets for each library functional area, including:

- Name, function, and square footage
- Occupants, equipment, furniture, and storage capacity
- Acoustics, computers, equipment, lighting, shelving, security systems, wiring, and flexibility
- Area relationships

Several examples of completed Functional Area Sheets are provided at the end of this appendix (see Exhibits B-1 through B-7).

Recommendations

Exterior

As you walk toward the Middletown Library it is still apparent that there are two distinct buildings, a children's library and an adult library. However, the children's library viewed from outside seems vacant much of the time, and there is no exterior sign marking the children's library. The doors no longer function as an entrance. An attractive steel rainbow sculpture is obscured by overgrown bushes. It may be useful for the future to consider identifying this part of the library by an exterior sign or banner and perhaps even reopening the entrance at least for program access.

Library Entrance

Inside the library, the children's facility is entered from the left-hand rather than the right-hand set of doors. At this entry point, children's facility users are far from the children's entrance, and there is no sign large enough to direct them. Facility users must turn to the right, cutting across the line of people waiting to check out materials, and enter a narrow corridor.

Children's Area

The entrance corridor (see Figure B-1) bisects the two major parts of the children's room. If you turn to your right, you enter the program area through an attractive rainbow arch (see Figure B-2).

This is a vital children's program area, but much of the time it is vacant (see Figure B-3). It looks like an ugly empty room with a few tables and chairs and a storage and sink area. It also contains the children's librarian's office, a small bathroom, and stairs

Figure B-1
Entrance corridor bisecting the two sections of Children's Services at Middletown Public Library.

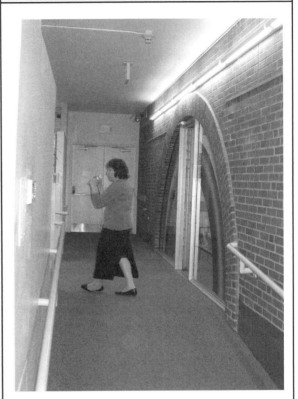

Figure B-2
Rainbow arch doorway (on right) that leads into the program area.

leading to the basement. An additional set of stairs leads up to nowhere! This large area offers an opportunity for a new, flexibly designed area for younger children that would increase the use of this part of the library.

Turning to the left, you enter the children's book stack and computer area, which is the heart of everyday children's library activities (see Figure B-4).

This part of the room can be entered by climbing a few steps (see Figure B-5) or by continuing down the corridor to a steep ramp (see Figure B-6). The ramp does not quite meet the handicapped accessibility requirement of a slope of 1 foot for every inch of vertical climb.

There are several distinct levels in the children's library:

- An entrance level
- A stairway or ramp up to the program area and book stacks
- Another ramp up to the courtyard level
- Stairs to a perch above this level

Between the stairs and ramp, on a platform above the corridor, is a large staff service complex (see Figure B-7). Staff object to the two access points (stairs and ramp; see Figure B-8), because their backs are to either the stairs or the ramp. They would prefer

Figure B-3
Empty craft area within the program area.

Figure B-4
The service desk and book stacks area.

to have a single handicapped accessible ramp as the entrance to this part of the room so they could welcome all visitors.

As you ascend the ramp and turn left into the library, you are greeted by a huge air-delivery unit (see Figure B-9). Behind that unit are closely spaced, tall book stacks, with narrow aisles made even narrower by several columns. The ceiling lighting is at an angle to the stacks.

To the rear of the stacks is an attractive group study room with four chairs (see Figure B-10). On the right of the entrance ramp there are several electronic workstations and tables and chairs. Bathrooms are to the right behind the computer area.

On the left there are some book stacks and a tall room with tall windows looking out into a courtyard (see Figure B-11). In this pleasant room are some book stacks, several lounge chairs and tables, a rocking chair, and a small play area with toys. At the end of the room, tall stairs lead to a small perch above the room (see Figure B-12).

**Figure B-5
Stair entry to the service desk and book stacks.**

**Figure B-6
Ramp entry to the service desk and book stacks.**

Figure B-7
Staff service complex.

Figure B-8
The two service desk access points—stairs and ramp.

The tall book stack and black bookcase behind the rail detract from the open view into the room (see Figure B-13). The children's services area is too crowded and small. Materials are crowded together, and there is little open space for children to move around. Book stacks are crowding out people space.

Several changes could improve services in this area. Simple changes requiring minimal rearranging of furniture include the following:

- Relocate younger children to the program area.
- Alternatively, relocate younger children to the area near the courtyard.
- Create a smaller staff service desk in the present location.
- Reconfigure and reduce book stacks to create wider aisles and avoid columns in aisles. Paint stacks a lighter color or at least paint stack tops.

**Figure B-9
Air delivery unit.**

**Figure B-10
Group study room.**

Figure B-11
High-ceilinged room with a view to the courtyard outside.

- Place book trucks with recently returned materials in front of appropriate stack range instead of using sorting shelves.
- Create a study area with carrels and tables.
- Use low book display units and lounge seating in this area.
- Place taller stacks in the rear.

Future changes requiring more extensive work include the following:

- Close off the small stairs at the entrance to create a single entrance so that staff can face users as they enter.
- Redesign the program area to create an activity area for younger children, and locate new mobile picture book bins in this area.
- Use cushions and wheelbarrow carrels for younger children.
- Consider moving staff work area to the program room.
- Improve lighting by using 30/30 fixtures and cork floors in the book stacks.
- Reconfigure ramp and stairs according to handicapped access specifications.
- Install higher intensity spotlighting for children's materials.

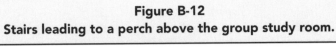

Figure B-12
Stairs leading to a perch above the group study room.

- Remove walls to create an open appearance.
- Reopen the exterior children's entrance, and identify the children's library from the exterior of the building.
- Inherent in the previous recommendations is a split in the area necessitated by the closed-off large program room.
- It may be useful to consider a major future redesign of the area that would create a larger open children's area that would integrate small and taller children, allowing for better staff utilization and control of children's activities. This plan would remove the walls separating these two areas.
- Build a library addition on the property next door to the existing children's room that was recently acquired by the library.

Figure B-13
Tall book stacks and black bookcase blocking the open view of the room.

Sample Functional Area Sheets

Exhibit B-1 **Functional area sheet: Small children and parenting area.**	
Name of area: Small Children and Parenting Area	**Dimensions: 900 sq. ft.**

Activities: Parents and younger children select materials, browse, and read.

Occupancy: Public 20

Major design features and ambience of area: Open activity space for children should be defined by picture book bins and shelving. Visual and acoustical separation from children's study area is essential. Child safety considerations such as rounded corners and protected electrical receptacles should be incorporated in the design. Sound-absorbing materials are essential. Lighting should emphasize the colorful book covers.

Furnishings and equipment:
Entrance and new materials
Display area with bulletin board
Displayers for 200 new materials
Space for parking strollers
Storage bins for backpacks
Activity area
- Play center with large interactive toys
- *Big books, puzzles, toys, games, blocks*

Parents' area
- 2 oversized adult lounge chairs for parent and child to read together
- *30 shelves for parent resources*

Study/research area
- 4 electronic workstations
- *2 tables with 4 chairs each*

Picture book area
- 170 bins/shelves for picture books and beginning readers; about 9,000 items
- *7 shelves for board books*
- Rocking chair

Seating:
Total of 15
- 2 oversized adult lounge chairs
- 1 rocking chair
- 4 ergonomic chairs for computer workstations
- 8 chairs for study tables

Materials:
200 shelves with picture books, beginner reader books, and parent resources
Bins for displaying picture books
Board books, big books, puzzles, games, toys, blocks

Proximity to: Entrance to children's room, service desk, story area restrooms
Distant from: Quiet areas, teens and adults

Exhibit B-2
Functional area sheet: Tall children/reference/nonfiction/fiction area.

Name of area: Tall Children/Reference/Nonfiction/Fiction	Dimensions: 1,700 sq. ft.

Activities: Older children and parents browse and look for particular books. Elementary school children research for homework assignments, use computers, and study.

Occupancy:
Public 12
Staff 2

Major design features and ambience of area:
Visually and acoustically separated from noisy areas
Task-lighted book stacks in one uniform pattern for easy finding of materials
Wide aisles, well-lighted, with subject signage
Displays interspersed within the stacks
Two small alcoves with seating for four in each
Good visibility from children's service area

Furnishings and equipment:
400 shelves of 66-inch-high shelving, ranges 18 feet long, double-faced book stacks for books
Lift display units for DVDs, CDs, audiotapes, computer software; to hold 500 units
20 shelves of reference books
Stack end panel displays
Magazine display racks for 25 titles
10 Spinners for paperbacks and media
2 PAC computers standup
2 tables for 4 each
12 electronic workstations with ergonomic task chairs
2 book carts with returned materials waiting to be shelved
Atlas/dictionary stand
Trash receptacle

Seating:
Total of 20
- 8 chairs for study tables
- 12 ergonomic task chairs for computer workstations

Materials:
400 shelves for books (100 Fiction, 300 Nonfiction, 36 Biography)
500 CDs, audiotapes, DVDs, computer software
9 shelves for magazines titles and back issues

Proximity to: Children's service desk

Exhibit B-3
Functional area sheet: Children's program room.

Name of area: Children's Program Room	**Dimensions: 800 sq. ft.**

Activities:
Preschool storyhour for 30 children, after-school and summer programs for 30 school-aged children, children's media presentations, and craft activities

Occupancy: 50 children and parents

Major design features and ambience of area:
Separate story and craft areas
Flexible for a variety of programs, such as storytelling, crafts, and play activities
Safe, warm, and friendly place for toddlers and preschool children; can also serve for elementary school
   programs and activities

Furnishings and equipment:

Visible through glass with curtains or shades	Capable of being darkened for media presentations
Acoustically separated from other children's areas	4 large tables for crafts, adjustable in height,
Craft area sink and counter with washable floor	light and portable
Several large storage closets	Cable TV hookup
Easily maintained floor coverings	Emergency exit
High-intensity lighting (70 foot-candles) with	Perimeter wall shelving
low glare	Story area with carpeted platform seating

Seating:
Public 50
Staff 1

Proximity to: Children's work area, children's picture and e-books, children's restrooms
Distant from: Adult areas, children's study and children's tall Reference, Nonfiction, and Fiction

Exhibit B-4
Functional area sheet: Children's group study room.

Name of area: Children's Group Study Room	**Dimensions: 200 sq. ft.**

Activities: Children study quietly in small groups.

Occupancy: Public 6

Major design features and ambience of area:

Visible through glass	White board on wall
Quiet, acoustically separated and dampened	Electrical receptacles (4) and low-voltage wired access

Furnishings and equipment:

Table and 6 chairs	Cable TV hookup
Capable of being darkened for media presentations	Perimeter wall shelving

Seating: Public 6

Proximity to: Book stacks, visible from staff service desk
Distant from: Small children's play area

Exhibit B-5
Functional area sheet: Children's services office.

Name of area: Children's Services Office	Dimensions: 150 sq. ft.

Activities: Children's librarian and staff work and meet.

Occupancy: Staff 6

Major design features and ambience of area:

Visible through glass	White board on wall
Quiet, acoustically separated and dampened	Electrical receptacles (4) and low-voltage wired access

Furnishings and equipment:

Desk with ergonomic chair	Cable TV hook-up
Electronic workstation	Perimeter wall shelving
Table and 4 chairs	Credenza
Capable of being darkened for media presentations	Files

Seating: Staff 5

Proximity to: Visible from staff service desk
Distant from: Small children's play area

Exhibit B-6
Functional area sheet: Children's staff work area.

Name of area: Children's Staff Work Area	Dimensions: 300 sq. ft.

Activities: Administrative duties, answer telephone, prepare materials for children's programs and displays, process children's materials.

Occupancy: Staff 4

Major design features and ambience of area:
Acoustically dampened
Task lighted
Work area with visibility to preschool areas
Support staff work areas with work space and storage for storyhour materials and equipment
Storage closet with deep shelving for program supplies and equipment

Furnishings and equipment:
Large counter with workstations for 5 staff
Storage for various equipment used to produce materials for children's displays
Lateral file cabinet with 4 drawers
Telephone
Clock
Trash receptacle

Seating: Staff 5

Materials: 2 book carts

Proximity to: Children's programs and small children's area

Exhibit B-7
Functional area sheet: Children's staff service desk.

Name of area: Children's Staff Service Desk	Dimensions: 100 sq. ft.

Activities: Reference service duties for children, parents, caregivers, and teachers, including technical assistance, telephone, interlibrary loan, and program registration

Occupancy: Staff 1

Major design features and ambience of area:
Acoustically dampened
Task lighted
Children's desk with visibility to the entire children's area

Furnishings and equipment:
Data tower or desk with chairs for staff and public
2 book carts
Photocopier and sorting shelf
Large display calendar listing children's events for the month

Seating:
Staff 1
Public 1

Materials: 2 book carts

Proximity to: Children's entrance

APPENDIX C

Large Children's Library Case Study: Children's Area Program for the Queens Borough Public Library

This appendix presents a case study of a larger city children's library designed for a new building on two levels and incoporating interactive and changing exhibits. The program implemented at the Queens Borough Public Library was prepared in close cooperation with the children's staff, Peter Magnani and his facility's staff, the architectural teams in the offices of Juergen Riehm and Tom Rockwell, and the staff of the San Francisco Exploratorium. The Children's Library Discovery Center design team met to discuss preliminary children's area design parameters. The following data were compiled and decisions made during the planning stages.

- Queens schoolchildren speak 140 different languages at home. Forty-six percent were born abroad, and 53 percent do not speak English at home.
- Books should be featured on each floor, with pictorial signage featuring subjects with Dewey Decimal numbers.
- Areas should be arranged by age:
  - An open area with book bins for preschool and kindergarten children designed with broad concepts, colors, shapes, letters, and opposites
  - Tables and chairs for first through third graders
  - Displays featuring words, the ABCs, counting sequences
  - Flexibility and study booths for fourth through sixth graders ("tweeners"); incorporate abstract concepts, pop culture, relationships
- Always show subjects with Dewey Decimal numbers, never numbers alone, so that children learn that Dewey numbers have consistent meanings.
- Arrange for staff to select especially useful books to go with the exhibits and duplicate purchases of these books so that there will always be some near the appropriate exhibits.

- Connect the two floors visually so that children always are conscious that there are two floors to the children's area. Create atrium, open stairwell?
- Exhibits should be consistently age appropriate.
- Safety consciousness is always important. Triple-padded carpets will be used at potential falling locations. Stair rails and banisters will be installed on stairways. All furnishings will have rounded edges.
- Be conscious of opportunities to introduce foreign languages—perhaps use non-Roman letters as displays.
- Install light, hanging curtains to gently suggest separation of age areas.
- Use as much natural lighting as possible on both floors. Use natural-spectrum artificial lighting.
- Staff need a very large storage area.

Children's Library Facility Planning

The children's services area should provide space for a full range of services and activities to promote and encourage learning, reading, and the enjoyment of books and other materials. The design and appearance of the children's room will make a lasting impression upon the child. The area should express warmth and friendliness and suggest to parent and child that this is the place to come in order to satisfy educational, information, and recreational needs.

Services and materials in this area must meet the needs of a range of library users, from the curious infant to the developing preteen with rapidly changing interests. It must also serve the needs of parents, childcare professionals, teachers, psychologists, and others who will use the children's collection to support their work with children.

Design Options

Children's facilities are often designed with playful concepts to attract children. Creative treatment of ceilings, doors, windows, and furnishings should provide a strong immediate message that this is a special place. However, libraries are special places in themselves. Books, videos, music, images, and words encourage children's imagination. These items themselves should be the decoration of the children's room.

A large train can contain picture book bins as cars in the train, but it should look more like a picture book bin than a freight train. A children's low platform overlooking the picture book train can hint at the captain's deck of an ocean liner, but trying too hard to make it into an actual ocean liner can look too cute and corny and become boring in time. Furnishings and equipment should encourage children's imagination to make them what they will. The platform can be a deck, a balloon floating in the sky, or a space station, depending on the child's imagination.

Express the character and history of the community with distinctive images. Classic and durable images should grace some of the walls of the children's areas where children can see them. Images should flow naturally from the library's function to stimulate the imagination and offer children a variety of materials and ways to experience these materials.

Make coat racks for children available near the multipurpose area as well as distributed throughout the area for convenient access to seating. Locate restrooms close to staff for supervision.

Height

Children grow at varying rates and psychologically change with chameleon-like speed, so pay close attention to these characteristics in the design of the room. Adult designers should try walking around on their knees to get some sense of how children will experience these spaces. Sixty-inch-high book stacks can seem like dark caverns to four-year-olds. Conversely, any opportunity to give children some height in the room will be welcome.

Displays

Changeable displays and seasonal decorations are an important aspect of the children's area. There will be tackable display walls in different parts of the room, as well as display cases.

Lighting

Controlled, natural lighting as well as indirect and diffuse ambient lighting will impart a quiet and cozy atmosphere by avoiding glare, but special adjustable spotlighting for materials and displays should provide strong visual punctuation for materials.

Openness and Quiet

Spatial density and the degree of openness present something of a design problem. The need to monitor children can conflict with the child's need for privacy.

Research into design options has produced somewhat contradictory and ambiguous results. Studies have shown that spatial density tends to increase aggression among preschool children. At the same time, open areas tend to result in running and cross-room talking. Research has also shown that activity areas with partitions tend to increase cooperative behavior. The answer may be low dividers between activity areas with higher dividers and increasing privacy for older children. Furnishings and dividers should always be low enough so that children can see and be seen by staff.

Children may seek relief from overactive open areas in quiet alcoves.

Flexibility and Mobile Furnishings

In the children's area there is the need to reconfigure the area for special programs or weekly displays. Flexibility will be enhanced by the following:

- Mobile multimedia display units with flat screens, books, display boards, and display shelving for quick setup of topics
- Low shelving on Darnell-Rose ball-bearing casters

- Sled-based chairs or chairs on casters that will glide easily (children may occasionally play bumper chairs, but the need for flexibility outweighs occasional discipline problems)
- Wireless wheelbarrow electronic workstations with two wheels and two legs, which allow for rapid relocation while retaining some stability
- Electrical and low-voltage receptacles distributed throughout the area; wall plugs at 36 inches off the floor with childproof guards
- Light fixture locations designed for task flexibility
- Acoustical adjustability by movable acoustical partitions and sound-dampening materials

Vestibule Entrance

The vestibule may include a display of children's art and community events. Provide a clearly organized orienting view from the entrance to the other children's service areas. There should be direct access to the story room and performance space from the entrance.

Developmental Areas

The children's room will have several distinct areas arranged to invite children and their caregivers to move through the space and the service it supports in accordance with the child's conceptual development. Because of the wide range of ages and things done here, there will be a noticeably different ambiance for these areas within the larger area. Transitional areas between each of these spaces will house services used common to both age groups, such as the computer Internet access area between preschool and elementary school areas. Visual access by staff is mandatory.

Each of the following areas discussed should serve as an imaginal landscape of the developmental period. The space should invoke a sense of containment for the projection and experience of the child's own imaginal field—a real field of dreams that encourages and supports a variety of imaginative feelings.

The sequence of areas should facilitate a successively more introverted relationship to the materials than the previous area so that the preschool child will be engaged with parents and staff while the intermediates and young adults will work more independently.

Infant, Toddler, and Preschool Area

This is a noisy, whimsical area for children two to five years old. A large bulletin board for children and a large, colorful clock will be visible from the entrance. Furnishings should have no sharp corners.

There are several collections of books in the preschool area:

- Bin shelves with alphabetical labels on each bin may hold picture books.
- A toddler section will have board books in colorful cubes.
- Big books will be housed in a sloping shelf display.

Seating will include the following:

- Oversized chairs for parents to read stories to their children
- Small tables and chairs (two sizes)
- Low floor tables with cushions

At some distance from the preschool area will be a platform with carpeted stairs for children to climb and a triple-padded carpeted area at the foot of the stairs. The edge of the stair should have a contrasting color, and there should be a ramp for handicapped access. This platform will be located carefully to avoid proximity to heavy traffic areas and to ensure safety of children.

Parenting, Professional, and Reference Area

Parents, teachers, childcare, and homeschool providers in addition to children will use this active but quiet area. It will contain:

- Reference and parenting collections near tables
- Collaborative electronic workstations to fit parent or librarian and child
- Tables and chairs
- Large oversized chair and a half so parents can read to their children here
- Tutorial rooms for individual consultation with children

Elementary Schoolers Intermediate Browsing/Reading

In a discussion with older children, they complained that children's rooms were designed for little kids and that there was no place for them. Therefore, differentiate this part of the room from the preschool spaces. This part of the children's area will suggest more contained behavior and more directed activity. It will include:

- Book stacks with wide aisles
- Display racks for new emergent-readers' books, juvenile Fiction and Nonfiction books, CDs, and videocassettes
- Display shelving for magazines and paperbacks
- A variety of seating and table heights
- Electronic workstations with embedded monitors

Study and homework area will include:

- A quiet area with chairs and tables for study
- Computers for database and Internet searching
- Copier with sorting counter
- Group study areas for four people each

Children's Multipurpose Area

The multipupurose area is where storyhours, craft activities, puppet shows, creative dramatics, parenting programs, discussions, author talks, book groups, and video viewing take place. The room should have acoustical separation to keep noise from entering other areas of the building. There will be several folding tables. Storage for chairs and tables will be useful. The story area may be carpeted. The activity area for crafts will have:

- Easily cleaned flooring, sink, counter
- Storage for materials
- Stackable chairs and tables
- Large format video screen

Multimedia and Audiovisual Facilities

The multimedia and audiovisual facilities are for viewing and listening to videos, music, and audiotapes individually and in small groups and for playing with games, puzzles, toys, and computer games. They will include computers with printers on lock-and-roll storage carts.

Restroom Facilities

There will be a unisex restroom for children located within the children's area and convenient to the program room. The room will include a toilet, sink, and changing table. There will also be a water fountain located nearby.

Staff Work Area

The children's service desk should be visible upon entering the children's area and should provide good supervision of the entire area. It will have sections for public service, including answering reference questions. There will be staff work locations at the desk, with computers, a printer, and a telephone. A large display calendar will list children's events for the month. The desk will include an alternative material checkout location for busy times of the day.

The staff work and storage area will have electronic workstations with Internet access, a printer, and an arts and crafts space with sink, design table, and counter for laminating equipment. Storage will hold posters, prints, mobiles, flannel boards, a puppet tree, and office supplies. The staff area will have operable windows and curtains, blinds, or shades to adjust for the privacy of workers within the staff work area.

The children's area office must provide good supervision of all children's activities. The staff should, however, be able to adjust privacy in the office by closing blinds on windows and the door. The office will include dividable space for the children's librarian. The workstation should allow observation of active areas. Working materials will be kept in adjustable shelves.

Young Adult Services

Library service needs of teenagers include space for social activities as well as space for age-appropriate materials and studying. Teens should feel that the library welcomes them and provides opportunities for them to socialize as well as study quietly. Locating teen services is often a puzzle. A location close to reference services provides the incentive to study, but a separate location requires additional staffing. Placing teens in the children's area would be discouraging to many teens. Close proximity to the attractive display of new materials, especially music, would be welcome.

Teens come to the library for several widely differing purposes. They will alternate between these very different sets of activities:

- They come to meet friends. This is a behavior pattern that libraries must design for if they are to be welcoming to this age group. An area designed for acoustical dampening of conversation, perhaps including a small coffee and snack service area, would be enjoyed by many teens.
- Teens often study in small groups so study areas for four to six people would be welcome.
- Music is very important for teens, especially music they can share.

These conflicting uses require careful acoustical design to allow noisy and quiet activities within this space, which in turn will be acoustically separated from other areas.

The recreational use area should emphasize constantly changing popular videos, audiotapes, books, and magazines on a flexible linear display system so that particular titles can be easily located. It should also include an art display area, bulletin boards easy to move around, comfortable lounge seating with low tables, and mobile viewing and listening stations with easily repaired or replaced equipment. It may be located near a food service area.

The study area should include the following:

- Oversize study tables with four chairs each
- Individual electronic workstations
- A place for coats and backpacks

This young adult area may have to be expanded and should be located and designed for considerable future flexibility. Additional staff may be needed if this teen area is expanded.

Young Adult Design Considerations

Ask teens what they want, and they will tell you:

- Alternating study and meeting areas
- Flexible size and furnishings
- Music opportunities
- Community board for events
- Homework help
- Large tables for interactive work
- Group study rooms or acoustical dampening
- Furnishings from Linea or other teen suppliers
- Special lighting effects

Design Result

The overall result of the children's area design should be an intriguing combination of creativity, function, and flexibility. Children should be engaged by areas that stimulate their imagination while suggesting a variety of behaviors. Alternating busy and quiet environments should offer children a choice. The area should be easy to change both for short-term display and long-term changes in function as children change. Parents and other caregivers should have an opportunity to sit with children to read to them and enjoy their reading skills. There should be an opportunity for individual consultation with children for teaching and discussion.

Some Final Thoughts

There are several works (of both authors and publishers) that would be particularly easy to use as the basis for connecting exhibits to books.

The Dorling Kindersley publishing company has an extensive range of titles for young adults, including books, CDs, and DVDs. In 1998, they published David Macaulay's *The New Way Things Work* on CD. Perhaps this CD could be connected with the "machine in motion plaza."

Walter Wick's enormously popular *I Spy* series and Richard Scarry's books may also give clues as to how children love to decode intricate pictures with many objects. I used Scarry's books with my own tutorial work with Vietnamese immigrants in the 1980s.

There are some interesting connections between science and art that children might explore. I am thinking of the catenary concept and Jasper Johns' current exhibit at the Matthew Marks Gallery in New York. Perhaps some ideas from aesthetic realism might fit in here.

On a really whacked-out level, what about the new bzzzpeek Web site (www. bzzzpeek.com) relating animals, action, and words?

Appendix D

Annotated List of Readings

This appendix provides a brief list of readings related to children's library design issues.

Baule, Steven. 2007. *Facilities Planning for School Library and Technology Centers*. Worthington, OH: Linworth Books. 134 pp.

> The author discusses how to remodel or build a new school library. He includes case studies from practitioners on common facilities issues, ready-to-use sample tools, and floor plans. He provides technological and practical information to make a functional, enduring, and accommodating library for the future, with checklists, forms, and timelines. To order: 480 East Wilson Bridge Road, Suite L, Worthington, OH, 43085.

Bolan, Kimberly. 2006. "Looks Like Teen Spirit: Libraries for Youth Are Changing—Thanks to Teen Input." *School Library Journal* 52 (November): 44–49.

> During the past ten years, many libraries have transformed their young adult areas into more efficient, innovative, and inspirational spaces. Many teens have suddenly found the library warm and inviting—a place that encourages independence, learning, socialization, and creativity. As more people learn about the positive impact of dynamic teen spaces, librarians want to know how they can make that happen in their own workplaces. This article provides a list of guidelines to help make teen spaces in libraries more teen-friendly.

Bryan, Cheryl. 2007. *Managing Facilities for Results: Optimizing Space for Services*. Chicago: ALA Editions, Public Library Association. 221 pp.

> This hands-on workbook discusses how to prioritize new services that need space, make plans, identify an appropriate location, present the case to funding authorities, conduct a "gap analysis," find resources to reallocate and see what new items are needed, and identify building professionals to assist with alterations. It is supplemented with 23 work forms to support the information and collection process. Three toolkits provide technical assistance on calculating square footage, assessing the message, and complying with the Americans with Disabilities Act (ADA) requirements. With examples ranging from small to large public libraries, the process is equally valuable for school, special, and academic librarians who are faced with similar space repurposing challenges.

Bugher, Kathryn M. 2006. "Design Considerations for School Library Media Centers." Madison: Wisconsin Department of Public Instruction. Available: http://dpi.state.wi.us/imt/desgnlmc .html.

> Bugher delineates ideal adjacencies, layout, communication networks, television distribution, data networking, electrical design, acoustics, ADA guidelines, size recommendations, and shelving calculations.

Celano, Donna, and Susan B. Neuman. 2001. "The Role of Public Libraries in Children's Literacy Development: An Evaluation Report." Harrisburg: Pennsylvania Library Association. Available: www.statelibrary.state.pa.us/libraries/lib/libraries/Role%20of%20Libraries.pdf.

In this Wisconsin Library Services and Technology Act–funded report, Drs. Celano and Neuman describe the ways in which public libraries foster literacy skills through summer reading programs and preschool programs. Recent literature they studied showed:
- Libraries continue to play a major role in fostering literacy, especially among those most needing assistance in developing literacy skills (e.g., preschool and elementary school children).
- Children who have been exposed to library preschool programs showed a greater number of emergent literacy behaviors and pre-reading skills than those in a control group.
- Children who participate in summer reading programs benefit from the many literacy-related activities offered, aiding significantly in literacy development.
- Public library preschool and summer reading programs encourage children to spend a significant amount of time with books.

Dewe, Michael. 1995. *Planning and Designing Libraries for Children and Young People*. Lanham, MD: Bernan Associates. 227 pp.

This book focuses on "space as a resource," covering such topics as types of space provision in both school and public libraries, the stages involved in creating space, and the practical concerns of planning new spaces. It includes case studies of completed libraries, library plans and photographs, and appendices of information, furniture, and equipment resources.

Erikson, Rolf, and Carolyn Markuson. 2001. *Designing a School Library Media Center for the Future*. Chicago: American Library Association. 109 pp.

This booklet presents guidance on building superior school library media centers by outlining conceptual plans from actual school libraries and explaining how to address specific planning and operational issues. The booklet discusses how to address the unique ergonomic and technology needs of children; how to control costs using proven bidding and evaluation methods; how to understand the technical drawings and language used in architecture; and how to limit liability while creating universal ADA compliance access. Appendices provide the common architectural symbols, suggested space allocations and adjacencies, a sample area data form, general information on shelving, chair and table heights, sample furniture specifications, and a list of furniture manufacturers.

Feinberg, Sandra, Kathleen Deerr, Barbara A. Jordan, Marcellina Byrne, and Lisa G. Kropp. 2007. *The Family Centered Library Handbook*. New York: Neal-Schuman. 200 pp.

This handbook on how to create a family-centered library contains tips and techniques for engaging and involving parents and caregivers in helping children develop literacy skills. Topics include using library resources to support parents and caregivers in guiding their children's growth and development; helping children's librarians interact successfully with families; implementing communication strategies, appropriate services, and useful spaces for adult/child participation; how to attract new and diverse families; and how to build community visibility.

Feinberg, Sandra, and Joan F. Kuchner. 1998. *Learning Environments for Young Children: Rethinking Library Spaces and Services*. Chicago: American Library Association. 196 pp.

The first section covers the theories and practices for librarians to provide social and physical environments in which parents, administrators, and the community work together with young children. The second section describes the methodologies, strategies, and tools for an "Early Childhood Quality Review" (ECQR), a self-evaluation process. The third section gives replicable questionnaires, observation guides, and other documentation aids necessary to evaluate spaces, programs, and resources.

Feinberg, Sandra, and Diantha D. Schull. 2000-2001. "Transforming Public Libraries to Serve Very Young Children and Their Families." Family Place Libraries. Available: www.familyplace libraries.org/documents/zerotothreearticle-1.pdf.

> This article describes the Family Place Library model by discussing the key features of this type of library: the Parent/Child Workshop, specially designed spaces and collections, and specially trained staff who engage in coalition building, community outreach, and professional development.

Fine, Jerold W. 2001. *Building Blocks for Planning Functional Library Space*. Chicago: Library Administration and Management Association, Building and Equipment Section Facilities Committee. 30 pp.

> This publication provides detailed formulas to help calculate the square footage required for every conceivable element of a library building. It includes specifications for computer workstations and visual representations of complex configurations.

Gisolfi, Peter. 1998. "A Place to Read." *American School Board Journal* 185, no. 10 (October): 35–37.

> To integrate the library fully into the educational life of an elementary school, the following design principles are offered: (1) locate the library centrally within the school, (2) provide separate areas for different functions, (3) design the entire space so that it can be observed by one adult, and (4) incorporate computers seamlessly into the library environment.

Gisolfi, Peter. 2003. "School Libraries: At the Center of the School." *School Planning and Management* 42, no. 12 (December): 28–29.

> Gisolfi describes three projects in which new school libraries were built within existing facilities, transferring them from the extremities to a central place, integrating them into the curriculum, and making them the focus of the school.

Graham, Carole. 2005. "Furniture for Libraries." Libris Design, funded by The Institute of Museum and Library Services, Washington, DC. Available: www.librisdesign.org/docs/Furniture Libraries.pdf.

> Graham discusses a library furniture program, procurement methods, furniture selection, materials selection, furniture types, and furniture installation. She includes a glossary of furniture terminology and further sources of information.

Hart, Thomas. 2006. *The School Library Media Facilities Planner*. New York: Neal-Schuman. 266 pp.

> Hart advises on preplanning, planning, designing, and redesigning a school media center. Architectural styles and terminology, sample floor plans, planning documents, contracts, bid requests, organizational worksheets, and lists of references and resources are included. Factors that distinguish elementary, middle, and secondary media centers are also considered.

Kaufman, J., ed. 1959. *Illuminating Engineering Society Lighting Handbook*. 3rd ed. New York: Illuminating Engineering Society.

> Known as the "Bible of Lighting," this manual explains the concepts, techniques, application, procedures, and systems of professional lighting installation. It includes definitions, charts and diagrams, as well as other illustrations.

Livingston, Heather. 2007. "Nine Libraries Called Out for Design Excellence." AIA Architect. Available: www.aia.org/aiarchitect/thisweek07/0406/0406d_library.cfm.

> The 2007 American Institute of Architects/American Library Association Awards recognized nine exceptionally planned and design projects, including a philanthropic elementary school library renovation.

Malman, David. 2005. "Lighting for Libraries." Libris Design, funded by The Institute of Museum and Library Services Available: www.librisdesign.org/docs/LightingLibraries.pdf.

> The most important issues in lighting design for libraries include light sources, lighting for book stacks, lighting in general reading and staff areas, day lighting, exterior lighting, lighting controls, accessibility issues, and good architectural design.

Myerberg, Henry. 2002. "School Libraries: A Design Recipe for the Future." American Library Association. Available: www.ala.org/ala/aasl/aaslpubsandjournals/kqweb/kqarchives.

> Myerberg discusses the design elements of a twenty-first-century school library, including space, books and shelving, seats, tables, technology (computers, scanners, projectors), building materials (wood, metal, plastic, paint, glass, fibers), and light and color. A sidebar describes the L!brary Initiative to creatively design, professionally staff, and technologically equip New York City's public elementary school libraries.

Sannwald, William W. 2001. *Checklist of Library Building Design Considerations*. Chicago: Library Administration and Management Association. 200 pp.

> This book contains 1,500 questions to ask during the design phase of a new or remodeled library building project. Every aspect of library facility space and functions is addressed, from site selection and security to shelving and groundbreaking ceremonies. It includes design and architectural changes brought about by computer workstations and networks and a section on ADA requirements.

Scherer, Jeffrey. 1999. "Light and Libraries." *Library Hi Tech* 17, no. 4: 358–371.

> Scherer discusses light basics, the light spectrum, light measurement, reflectance, glare and brightness ratio, day lighting, electric lighting, and computer screens and lighting. He includes a checklist for plan review.

Schibsted, Evantheia. 2005. "Way Beyond Fuddy-Duddy: New Libraries Bring Out the Best in Students." Edutopia. Available: www.edutopia.org/design.

> Schibsted describes the work of the Robin Hood Foundation in redesigning 46 New York City school libraries during the years 2002–2005. The foundation engaged local architectural firms, which redesigned existing libraries and alternative spaces into whimsical and attractive settings. The creative flourishes of their work are emphasized in text and photographs.

Sonenberg, Nina. 2005. "Family Place Libraries: From One Long Island Library to the Nation." Americans for Libraries Council. Available: www.familyplacelibraries.org/documents/Portrait_FamilyPlace.pdf.

Underhill, Paco. 1999. *Why We Buy*. New York: Simon & Schuster.

> This book, based on the author's field research, examines the motivations behind consumer behavior in retail stores. He discusses such marketing ploys as product placement, aisle width, signage, and packaging and how these affect consumer purchases. Underhill also offers tips on how to adapt to changing consumer dynamics.

Wrightson, Denelle, and John M. Wrightson. 1999. "Acoustical Considerations in Planning and Design of Library Facilities." *Library Hi Tech* 17, no. 4: 349–357.

> Topics include intrusive noises, overly reverberant spaces, lack of speech privacy, sound transmission class, noise criteria, reverberation time and noise reduction coefficient, space planning, sound systems, and external noise.

APPENDIX E

Suppliers

This appendix provides contact information for some common American suppliers of library furnishings and equipment, arranged by type. For readers in the United Kingdom and Europe, please refer to this online resource updated daily by CILIP: www.buyers guideonline.co.uk/. It provides an up-to-date source on information on library suppliers' products and services in the United Kingdom.

Acoustical Equipment

Acoustical Surfaces
123 Columbia Court North, Suite 201
Chaska, MN 55318
800-448-0121
www.acousticalsurfaces.com
Equipment for monitoring noise levels,
Quiet Light™

Book Trucks

Darnell-Rose Casters
17915 Railroad St.
City of Industry, CA 91748
626-912-3765
www.casters.com
Book trucks and furniture

Eustis Chair
PO Box 842
Ashburnham, MA 01430
978-827-3103
www.eustischair.com
Epoxy-injected joints for fine chairs and book trucks

See also **General Equipment**

Chairs and Seating Units

Steel

American Seating
401 American Seating Center
Grand Rapids, MI 49504
800-748-0268
www.americanseating.com
Meeting room chairs

Design Within Reach
455 Jackson St.
San Francisco, CA 94111
800-944-2233
www.dwr.com
Modern furniture

Ekornes, Inc.
615 Pierce St.
Somerset, NJ 08873
732-302-0097
www.ekornes.com
Norwegian lounge chairs, the Stressless®
chair, high-back leather swivel chairs

Fixtures Furniture
1642 Crystal Ave.
Kansas City, MO 64126
800-821-3500
www.fixturesfurniture.com
Office chairs

Herman Miller, Inc
855 East Main Ave.
Zeeland, MI 49464
888-443-4357
www.hermanmiller.com
Aeron chairs

Krueger International
1330 Bellevue St.
Green Bay, WI 54302
414-468-8100
http://ki-inc.com
Perry Stack Chairs

Steelcase
PO Box 1967
Grand Rapids, MI 49501
616-247-2716
http://steelcase.com
Sensor® and Criterion® chairs, Uno by
Turnstone

Vecta Contract
1800 South Great Southwest Parkway
Grand Prairie, TX 75051
972-641-2860
www.vecta.com
Stacking chairs

Virco Manufacturing
2027 Harper's Way
Torrance, CA 29501
1-800-448-4726
www.virco.com
Comfortable steel stacking chairs

Wieland Furniture
13737 Main St.
PO Box 1000
Grabill, IN 46741
888-943-5263
www.wielandfurniture.com
Upholstered Loop, high-density foam
covered with Velcro-fastened covers for easy
reupholstering

Wooden

Aalto.com
6160 Olson Memorial Hwy
Golden Valley, MN 55422
866-517-5177
www.aalto.com
Aalto stools

CF Group
10650 Gateway Blvd.
St. Louis, MO 63132
314-991-9200
www.thefalconcompanies.com
Thonet chairs

Eustis Chair
PO Box 842
Ashburnham, MA 01430
978-827-3103
www.eustischair.com
"Z" chairs

Fetzer Architectural Woodwork
6223 West Double Eagle Circle
Salt Lake City Utah 84118
801-484-6103
www.fetzersinc.com
Wooden furniture

Huston & Company
226 Log Cabin Road
Kennebunkport, ME 04046
888-869-6370
http://hustonandcompany.com
Wooden chairs and tables

Lyndon Furniture
135 Industrial Parkway
Lyndon, VT 05849
802-748-0100
www.vermontmadefurniture.com
Wooden chairs and tables

Sauder Manufacturing Company
930 West Barre Rd.
Archbold, OH 43502
800-537-1530
www.saudermfg.com
Wooden chairs

Thos. Moser Cabinetmaker
PO Box 1237
72 Wrights Landing
Auburn, ME 04211
800-708-9045
http://thosmoser.com
Wooden furniture

See also **General Equipment**

Children's Furniture

Agati
1219 W. Lake St.
Chicago, IL 60607
312-829-1977
http://agati.com
Furniture for centers of learning

Gressco
328 Moravian Valley Rd.
Waunakee, WI 53597
800-345-3480
www.gresscoltd.com
Library and children's furniture

See also **General Equipment**

Circulation and Reference Desks

Fetzer Architectural Woodwork
6223 West Double Eagle Circle
Salt Lake City Utah 84118
801-484-6103
www.fetzersinc.com
Library furniture

See also **General Equipment**

Custom Design

Burgeon Group
2244 N. 13th St.
Phoenix, AZ 85006
602-451-7285
www.burgeongroup.com
Specializes in interactive learning spaces
incorporating large letters

Displayers

Beemak Plastics, Inc.
13921 Bettencourt Street
Cerritos, CA 90703
800-421-4393
www.beemak.com
Plastic displayers

Brodart
280 North Road
Clinton County Industrial Park
McElhattan, PA 17748
888-820-4377
www.brodart.com
Library supplies

Display Fixtures
PO Box 7245
Charlotte, NC 28217
800-737-0880
www.displayfixtures.com
Inexpensive painted plywood display fixtures

Franklin Fixtures
20 Patterson Brook Road
West Wareham, MA 02576
508-291-1475
www.franklinfixtures.com
Display fixtures

Library Display Design Systems
PO Box 8143
Berlin, CT 06037
860-828-6089
www.librarydisplay.com
Acrylic displayers

Library Display Shelving
173 West Ohio Ave.
Lake Helen, FL 32744
800-762-6209
www.librarydisplayshelving.com
Clear acrylic plastic displayers

MJ Industries
4 Carleton Drive
Georgetown, MA 01833
978-352-6190
www.mjshelving.com
Steel stacks and multimedia display systems

Showbest Fixture Corp.
PO Box 38366
Richmond, VA 23260
804-222-5535
http://showbest.com
Display fixtures

See also **General Equipment**

Electronic Workstations

Biomorph
11 Broadway, Space 10
New York, NY 10004
212-809-4323
http://biomorphdesk.com
Electronic workstations

Bretford, Inc.
11000 Seymour Ave.
Franklin Park, IL 60131
800-521-9614
www.bretford.com
Work space and electronic workstations

Nova Solutions, Inc.
421 W. Industrial Ave.
Effingham, IL 62401
217-342-7070
www.novadesk.com
Electronic workstations and embedded terminals

Paragon Furniture
2224 E. Randol Mill Rd.
Arlington, TX 76011
800-451-8546
www.paragoninc.com
Electronic workstations and embedded terminals

See also **General Equipment**

General Equipment

3M
3M Center
St. Paul, MN 55144
800-447-8826
http://soutions.3m.com
Book theft detection systems

Brodart
280 North Road
Clinton County Industrial Park
McElhattan, PA 17748
888-820-4377
www.brodart.com
General equipment and furnishings

Checkpoint Systems, Inc.
101 Wolf Drive
Thorofare, NJ 08086
800-257-5540
www.checkpointsystems.com
Theft detection and self-serve checkout systems

Control Concepts, Inc.
100 Park St.
Putnam, CT 06260
800-745-6551
www.ControlConceptsUSA.com
Manual counting devices

Creative Library Concepts
535 Boulevard
Kenilworth, NJ 07033
800-656-5401, x11
www.creativelibraryconcepts.com
Library furnishings

Educational Furniture, Inc.
15 Alden Street, Suite 7
Cranford, NJ 07016
800-545-4474
http://efurnitureinc.com
Kin-der-Link® stools

Gaylord Bros.
PO Box 4901
Syracuse, NY 13221
800-962-9580
www.gaylordmart.com
Library supplies and furniture

Gressco
328 Moravian Valley Rd.
Waunakee, WI 53597
800-345-3480
www.gresscoltd.com
Library and children's commercial furniture

Haworth, Inc.
One Haworth Center
Holland, MI 49423
800-344-2600
www.haworth.com
Office systems

Highsmith
W5527 State Road 106
PO Box 800
Fort Atkinson WI, 53638
800-558-2110
www.highsmith.com
General equipment and furnishings, school
chairs with changeable cushions

LCN Closers
121 West Railroad Ave.
PO Box 100
Princeton, IL 61356
800-526-2400
www.lcnclosers.com
Door closers designed for handicap
accessibility

Worden
199 East 17th St.
Holland, MI 49423
800-748-0561
www.wordencompany.com
General library furnishings

Lighting

Day-o-Lite
126 Chestnut St.
Warwick, RI 02888
401-467-8232
www.dayolite.com
Library stack lighting

Electrix, Inc.
45 Spring St.
New Haven, CT 06519
203-359-0230
www.electrix.com
Small desk lamps

George Kovacs Lighting
The Minka Group
1151 W. Bradford Ct.
Corona, CA 92882
951-735-9220
www.georgekovacs.com
Small lamps

Let There Be Neon
38 White St.
New York, NY 10013
212-226-4883
www.lettherebeneon.com
Neon lighting

Lighting by Gregory
158 Bowery
New York, NY 10012
800-807-1826
www.lightingbygregory.com
Table lamps

Luxo Corp.
200 Clearbrook Rd.
Elmsford, NY 10523
800-222-5896
www.luxous.com
Lighting and magnification products

Peerless Lighting
PO Box 2556
Berkeley, CA 94710
510-845-2760
www.peerless-lighting.com
Cylinder library lighting

Swivelier
600 Bradley Hill Rd.
Blauvelt, NY 10913
845-353-1455
www.swivelier.com
Screw-in light fixtures

Sylvan R. Shemitz Designs, Inc.
114 Boston Post Rd.
West Haven, CT 06516
203-931-4455
www.elliptipar.com
Elliptipar stack lights

Visa Lighting
1717 W. Civic Dr.
Milwaukee, WI 53209
800-772-8472
www.visalighting.com
Wall, ceiling, pendant, and table lighting

Moving Equipment

Rentacrate, Inc.
4226 Grace St.
Schiller Park, IL 60176
800-427-2832
www.rentacrate.com
Rental moving equipment

Starnet Commercial Flooring
888-708-9753
www.starnetflooring.com
Liftman book stack moving systems

Shelving

Library Bureau
172 Industrial Road
Fitchburg, MA 01420
800-221-6638
www.librarybureau.com
Wooden furniture

MJ Industries
4 Carleton Drive
Georgetown, MA 01833
978-352-6190
www.mjshelving.com
Steel shelving

Tennsco
PO Box 1888
Dickson, TN 37056
800-251-8184
www.tennsco.com
Steel bracket shelving

See also **General Equipment**

Tables

Adden Furniture
26 Jackson St.
Lowell, MA 01852
800-625-3876
www.addenfurniture.com
Butcher block style

Mitchell Furniture Systems
1700 W. St Paul Ave.
PO Box 1156
Milwaukee, WI 53201
800-290-5960
www.mitchell-tables.com
Folding tables

Thos. Moser Cabinetmaker
PO Box 1237
72 Wrights Landing
Auburn, ME 04211
800-708-9045
http://thosmoser.com
Wooden tables

Tuohy Furniture
42 St. Albans Place
Chatfield, MN 55923
800-533-1696
www.tuohyfurniture.com
Wooden furniture

See also **General Equipment**

Toys and Blocks

Habermaass Corp.
4407 Jordan Rd.
Skaneateles, NY 13152
800-468-6873
www.habausa.com
Large, beautifully made wooden blocks and
toys from Germany

APPENDIX F

Architects

This appendix provides contact information for architects with whom the author has worked on various library projects. Local architects can best be researched by contacting state libraries, especially in those states that have library construction funds. Visiting well-designed libraries and asking for architectural references is another useful way of identifying architects. The Library Administrative and Management Association (LAMA) of the American Library Association also publishes a list of architects who have worked on libraries, but this is not a very selective list.

1100 Architect
Jurgen Riehm
435 Hudson St.
New York, NY 10014
212-645-1011

AnnBeha Architects
Pamela Hawk and Anne-Sophie Divenyi
33 Kingston St.
Boston, MA 02111
617-338-3000

Arbonies King Vlock
Glenn Arbonies
199 South Montowese St.
Branford, CT 06405
203-483-9900
Libraries: Glastonbury and Killingworth, CT

Centerbrook Architects
67 Main St.
Centerbrook, CT 06409
860-767-0175
Libraries: Quinnipiac College, East Hampton CT;
East Lyme, CT

Collins & Scoville Architects
40 Beaver St.
Albany, NY 12207
518-463-8068

Crown Street Architects
George Buchanan
341 Crown St.
New Haven, CT 06511
203-787-4896
Library: Branford, CT

Diseroad Wolff Kelly Clough Bucher, Inc.
Jay Clough and Bob Kelly
8 West Broad St.
Hatfield, PA, 19440
215-368-5806
Libraries: King of Prussia, PA; Moravian College,
Bethlehem, PA

Eck | MacNeely
Jeremiah Eck
560 Harrison Ave., Suite 403
Boston, MA 02118
617-367-9696

Fletcher Harkness Cohen Moneyhun • Stopfel
(formerly The Architects Collaborative)
46 Waltham St.
Boston, MA 02118
617-695-9300
Libraries: Yonkers, NY (design); Stuart, FL;
Liverpool, NY (in progress); Hartford, CT (in
progress)

Gustavson & Verelley Architect
144 Riverview Place
Stratford, CT 06497
203-375-8870
Libraries: Wallingford, Groton, and Fairfield, CT

J. Stewart Roberts Associates
48 Grove St.
Somerville, MA 02144
617-666-8585

JCJ Architects
Barbara Joslin
38 Prospect St.
Hartford, CT 06103
860-247-9226

Kaestle Boos Associates
416 Slater Road
PO Box 2590
New Britain, CT 06050
203-229-0361
Libraries: Newington and Easton, CT

Kevin Hom + Andrew Goldman Architects
45 East 20th St., 7th Floor
New York, NY 10003
212-777-0006

KSS Architects
Allan Kehrt
337 Witherspoon St.
Princeton, NJ 08542
609-921-1131

Lerner | Ladds + Bartels
Drayton Fair
236 Hope St.
Providence, RI 02906
401-421-7715

Michael Shilale Architects
Michael Shilale
140 Park Ave
New City, NY 10956
845-708-9200

Peter Gisolfi Associates
566 Warburton Ave.
Hastings on Hudson, NY 10706
914-478-3677
Libraries: Briarcliff Manor, Glens Falls, and
Bronxville, NY

Remick Architects & Planners
Conrad Remick
2 Executive Drive
New Windsor, NY 12550
914-564-5677
Libraries: Cornwall on Hudson (plans), Highland
Falls, NY

Robinson Green Beretta
Eric Johnson
50 Holden St.
Providence, RI 02908
401-272-1730
Libraries: Killingly, CT; Warwick, Woonsocket, and
Cranston, RI

Rockwell Architecture, Planning and Design
Henry Myerberg
5 Union Square West
New York, New York 10003
212-463-0334

Richard Schoenhardt
2 Tunxis Road
Tariffville, CT 06081
860-658-4496
Libraries: Middletown, NY; Somers, Essex,
Prospect, CT

Tappe Associates
Jeff Hoover
6 Edgerly Place
Boston, MA 02116
617-451-0200
Libraries: Milford, CT; Abington, Beverly Newton,
Natick, Methuen, and Worcester, MA; Keene, NH

Tuthill and Wells, Architects
Avon Park
North Avon, CT 06001
860-677-0660
Libraries: Preston, Washington, Mystic, Newtown,
and Groton, CT

**Woodward, Connor, Gillies & Seleman
Architects**
Bill Connor
20 Corporate Woods Blvd.
Albany, NY 12211
518-434-2556

Glossary

The terms defined here are also discussed within the text of the book. They are collected here with brief definitions for easy reference. For additional clarification, refer back to the chapter discussions.

active zone: Often located near an entrance, an open area that encourages activity and interaction among library patrons; may include play space, areas for conversation, and collaborative workstations.

ADA: Americans with Disabilities Act; dictates the federal guidelines for handicap accessibility in public and commercial buildings.

ambient lighting: A level of lighting that provides general illumination with low glare; often achieved using perimeter lighting units and hanging lamps.

anime: A form of Japanese hand- or computer-drawn cartoon animation.

assignable space: Those portions of a building that are designed for public or staff functions, often with furniture and equipment, and used for programmed activities.

balanced scorecard model: A technique for measuring whether an organization's short-term activities match its long-term goals by focusing on four perspectives: financial, customer, internal process, and learning and growth.

behavior mapping: In libraries, a technique used to describe the relative functions of the different spaces within the building by observing the types and frequencies of activities as well as the furnishings and equipment available, with defined areas; these observations are then plotted on maps for comparison.

book trucks: Carts used by library staff for storage and reshelving of books returned to the library.

carrel: A partitioned or enclosed table suitable for one person that is generally used for studying; when constructed with two wheels and two legs for easy relocation, known as a wheelbarrow carrel.

caster: One in a set of wheels designed for easy movement of furniture and equipment.

color rendering index (CRI): A measure of the ability of a light source to reproduce the colors of various objects faithfully in comparison with a natural light source.

demographic analysis: A technique used to measure the dimensions and dynamics of a population to determine how it changes over time, and a useful tool for estimating areas of growing need for specific services; in library design, it focuses on education, population growth, economics, and cultural characteristics.

end cap or **end panel:** Used to cover the ends of stack ranges.

Experience Library model: A twenty-first-century library model that focuses on creating a hands-on, dynamic, multimedia learning experience for library patrons, especially children; common elements include themed spaces, interactive exhibits, as well as spontaneous and planned programming.

Family Place Library model: A library initiative of Family Place Libraries that focuses on providing a nurturing environment for both children and caregivers by offering early childhood and parent services that support emergent literacy.

flexibility fallacy: The incorrect assumption that library functions are interchangeable and the particular functions do not have specific design requirements.

focus group: A representative group of people whose perceptions and attitudes are solicited as a means to gauge the needs of the larger population of interest; focus groups often suggest ideas that can then be further tested through surverys.

GASP: Brand creation strategy—graphics, ambience, style, presentation—based on a hospitality industry marketing initiative that is being applied to library design.

gondola: A freestanding display unit often used to display CDs or DVDs at waist height.

hi-lo workstations: Desks designed to be adjustable from sitting to standing positions and for a variety of heights.

HVAC: Heating, ventilation, and air-conditioning.

LEED: Leadership in Energy and Environmental Design, part of the Green Building Rating System of the U.S. Green Building Council, provides the nationally accepted benchmarks for design, construction, and operation of green buildings, with a focus on five key areas: sustainable site development, water savings, energy efficiency, materials selection, and indoor environmental quality.

library consultant: An experienced coach familiar with the planning process who evaluates existing library space and services to determine building objectives; the consultant writes the building program, with staff assistance, and reviews the schematic design plans.

manga: Japanese comics or print cartoons.

maximum use study: Technique used to determine the times when use of library facilities is at its peak; specific time-use patterns are charted and compared against total open hours.

mezzita: A height-adjustable, fixed-position electronic workstation that can accommodate multiple computers and users.

mission statement: A definition of an organization's purpose or objectives, often including a specific goal to work toward and the steps necessary to achieve that goal.

mobile display carts: Often constructed of steel with locking castor wheels for easy transport and stability, these shelving units allow for easy cover-out display of multimedia materials, such as videos, CDs, DVDs, and paperbacks.

needs assessment: An in-depth analysis of a current situation to identify areas needing improvement.

nonassignable space: Those portions of a building that are infrastructure and therefore not available for the provision of services; for example, entrance and vestibule, walls, restrooms, stairs and elevators, hallways, delivery, and storage areas.

picture rails: A strip of molding or other material from which pictures or art may be hung or mounted without hammering nails into the walls; allows for easy changes in decorations.

planning team: In library design, a group convened to determine the nature and direction of building renovation; typically composed of community members, library staff, the library consultant, an architect, and an interior designer.

quiet zone: An area often designated for long-term quiet study; often includes subdued lighting, calming colors, and individual study carrels.

ranges: A connected series of 3-foot shelving sections; often composed of six sections and averaging 18 feet long.

Robin Hood Library model: An initiative of the Robin Hood Foundation that seeks to transform run-down elementary school libraries into active learning centers to help address both low literacy and weak student performance among children from low-income households.

sight lines: An imaginary line extending from one's eye to the object or area being viewed. Unobstructed sight lines allow for careful monitoring of children and activities within different library areas.

signage: A system of signs used as a means of identification, instruction, or direction.

slat wall: A display system that allows for a variety of attachments for displaying materials.

sled-based chair: A chair designed with front and back legs that connect on each side, like sled runners, for easy mobility on carpeted flooring.

stacks: Multiple bookshelves arranged as a continuous structure to allow efficient storage of books; may also act as sound-absorbing barriers between library areas.

stimulus shelters: Quiet areas separated from open, active areas, providing shelter from overstimulation for children.

street presence: Having an exterior façade that attracts people walking by on the street, giving them an idea of what goes on inside and enticing them to enter.

SWOT analysis: A strategic planning technique that evaluates an organization's strengths, weaknesses, opportunities, and threats to determine the internal and external factors that could facilitate or hinder achieving objectives.

task lighting: A type of illumination that focuses directly on functional areas, such as displays, reading surfaces, and lounge seating; often achieved through the use of floor lamps, table lamps, or recessed ceiling fixtures that can be adjusted by users.

tracking studies: A technique for observing user behavior over time to determine how people use particular services and whether potential patterns in behavior exist.

vision statement: A vivid description of a desired outcome that reflects the values of an organization; for libraries, the vision statement often focuses on the look and feel of library services.

Vocera device: A wearable communication device that resembles a walkie-talkie and enables staff to maintain contact throughout the building.

Wi-Fi zone: An area that is covered by a wireless Internet connection.

WOW Library model: Based on a marketing and brand-creation strategy aimed at creating a unique library identity, this model focuses on three main components: the external environment, the library's internal environment, and marketing strategy to create the "brand."

zone: An area set off from other areas and designated as having a specific function.

Index

Page numbers followed by "i" indicate an illustration.

About the Author

During the past 36 years, Nolan Lushington has worked with over 200 libraries as a library consultant. He has been chairman of the American Library Association Buildings and Equipment section and a juror on the joint ALA/American Institute of Architects Building Awards Program. Mr. Lushington was a Council on Library Resources Fellow and, with Anthony Tappe, he has taught the summer workshop in Public Library Design at the Harvard University Graduate School of Design for the past 19 years. For over two decades, Mr. Lushington was the Director of the Greenwich Public Library in Connecticut, and for 11 years was Associate Professor at the library school at Southern Connecticut State University. He is married to Louise Blalock, Chief Librarian at Hartford Public Library and 2001 Library Journal Librarian of the Year, and has 7 children and 11 grandchildren. Mr. Lushington also wrote *Libraries Designed for Users* (Neal-Schuman, 2002), first published in 1979 and in print for 20 years.